D1795691

Dylan Thomas

Georgia Southern University

Jack N. and Addie D. Averitt Lecture Series

No. 6

Dylan Thomas

An Original Language

BARBARA HARDY

The University of Georgia Press

Athens and London

© 2000 by the University of Georgia Press
Athens, Georgia 30602
All rights reserved
Designed by Sandra Strother Hudson
Set in Cycles with Arepo display by G&S Typesetters, Inc.
Printed and bound by Maple-Vail Book Manufacturing Group
The paper in this book meets the guidelines for permanence and durability
of the Committee on Production Guidelines for Book Longevity of the
Council on Library Resources.
Printed in the United States of America
04 03 02 01 00 C 5 4 3 2 1

Library of Congress Cataloging-in-Publication Data
Hardy, Barbara Nathan.
Dylan Thomas : an original language / Barbara Hardy.
    p. cm. — (Jack N. and Addie D. Averitt lecture series ; no. 6)
Includes bibliographical references and index.
ISBN 0-8203-2207-5 (alk. paper)
1. Thomas, Dylan, 1914–1953—Criticism and interpretation.   2. Wales—
In literature.   I. Title.   II. Series.
PR6039.H52 Z669   2000
821'.912—dc21   99-057978

British Library Cataloging-in-Publication Data available

Collected Poems: Copyright 1938, 1939, 1943, 1946 © 1971 by New Directions
Publishing Corporation. Copyright 1953 by Dylan Thomas. Copyright ©
1937, 1955, 1956, 1957, 1962, 1966, 1967 by The Trustees for the Copyrights of
Dylan Thomas.

The Filmscripts: Copyright © 1966 by New Directions Publishing Corporation. Copyright 1942, 1946 © 1964 by The Trustees for the Copyrights of
Dylan Thomas.

Portrait of the Artist as a Young Dog: Copyright 1940 by New Directions Publishing Corporation.

Quite Early One Morning: Copyright 1954 by New Directions Publishing
Corporation.

The Broadcasts: Copyright 1951 © 1991 by The Trustees for the Copyrights of
Dylan Thomas.

The Poems of Dylan Thomas: Copyright 1938, 1939, 1943, 1946 © 1971 by New
Directions Publishing Corporation. Copyright 1953 by Dylan Thomas. Copyright © 1937, 1955, 1956, 1957, 1962, 1966, 1967 by The Trustees for the Copyrights of Dylan Thomas.

Under Milk Wood: Copyright 1954 by New Directions Publishing Corporation.

Poetry and Prose by Dylan Thomas used by permission of New Directions
Publishing Corporation.

TO AERONWY THOMAS

Contents

Foreword, ix

Preface, xi

Abbreviations, xv

1. The Regional Poet, 1

2. The Modernist Poet: The Stream that is Flowing
   All Ways, 31

3. Dramatic, Narrative, Lyric: Across the
   Genres, 51

4. The Reflexive Poet: The Theme of Art, 85

5. The Green Poet: The Theme of Nature, 132

Notes, 151

Index, 153

Foreword

In October 1995, Georgia Southern University and the Statesboro community were privileged to hear internationally renowned scholar Barbara Hardy deliver three lectures on the poetry and prose of her countryman, Dylan Thomas. Those lectures, centering on Professor Hardy's appreciation for Thomas as an innovator in language, form the substance of this present volume, which is dedicated to Aeronwy Thomas, the poet's daughter and Barbara Hardy's friend.

Barbara Hardy, Professor Emeritus of English Literature at Birkbeck College, University of London, and Honorary Professor of English, University of Wales, Swansea, has written extensively on the English novel and has published books on Austen, Thackeray, Dickens, and Eliot. A novelist herself, she has written *London Lovers* as well as a memoir, *Swansea Girl.* Actively "retired," Professor Hardy is pursuing ongoing study in Shakespeare, Dickens, Eliot, Hardy, Henry James, and James Joyce. She has lectured and held visiting professorships around the world, including Canada, Germany, Sweden, Russia, Poland, and Israel. We at Georgia Southern counted ourselves fortunate to host this remarkable critic, author, and teacher.

Professor Hardy's lectures were made possible through the generosity of Jack N. and Addie D. Averitt, who established the Averitt Lectures in 1990, as a gift to the Department of History and the Department of English and Philosophy, which host the lectures in alternating years. The Department of English has had the privilege of presenting James Olney, who lectured on the poetry of Whitman, Dickinson, and Hopkins; as well as Tony Tanner, who spoke on the nonfiction prose of Henry James. Barbara Hardy's 1995 lectures were followed in 1997 by those of Houston Baker, who addressed African American writers Booker T. Washington, W. E. B. Du Bois, Richard Wright, and Ralph Ellison. We thank Dr. and Mrs. Averitt, whose commitment to Georgia Southern has brought such distinguished scholars to the Statesboro community.

As Chair of the Averitt Lecture Committee for 1995, I have many people to thank. First I thank Karen Orchard and Jane Kobres at the University of Georgia Press for their help in seeing this book through to publication. I also thank the members of the Averitt Lecture Committee: Pat Ingle Gillis, Patsy Griffin, Dale Purvis, Candy B. K. Schille, and Terry Thompson. They were all generous with their time and cheerfully managed the many behind-the-scenes tasks that helped make Professor Hardy's visit to Georgia Southern run so smoothly. They deserve most credit for giving those days in October 1995, the illusion of effortless southern hospitality. Thanks also to Virginia Spell, whose gorgeous floral arrangements added so much elegance to the lecture platform and the reception tables. To John Humma and Helen Cannon, thanks for extending your hospitality to Dr. Hardy.

Finally, I thank Barbara Hardy herself for gracing us with her presence and for sharing with us her insights into the life and work of a poet for whom she has such an obvious affection. Because of Professor Hardy's lifelong dedication to the study of the literature that so enriches our lives, you have in your hand this book: *Dylan Thomas: An Original Language.*

DAVID DUDLEY
Chair, Averitt Lecture Committee, 1995

Preface

The core of this book is the Averitt lectures, 1995, given at Georgia Southern University. These lectures, revised and expanded, form the basis of the last three chapters and provide the title. I want to thank Dr. Jack N. Averitt and Mrs. Addie D. Averitt for their generous welcome and friendly presence; the members of the Averitt Lecture Committee who made my visit enjoyable, especially David Dudley, John Humma, and Patsy Griffin; and the Humma and Dudley families for their warm hospitality.

The first two chapters, on regionalism and modernism, are revised and much shortened forms of earlier pieces of work on Dylan Thomas: "Region and Nation: R. S. Thomas and Dylan Thomas," a lecture given at the first International Conference on Region and Nation at the University of Aberdeen and subsequently published in *The Literature of Region and Nation*, ed. R. P. Draper (Basingstoke: Macmillan, 1989), and the Gwyn Jones Lecture, delivered at Cardiff in May 1987, in the congenial presence of Gwyn Jones, printed by the University of Wales in 1987, and entitled *The Language of Dylan Thomas's Poetry: "The Stream that is flowing Both Ways."* I thank the University of Wales for permission to include this lecture here.

I am very grateful to Aeronwy Thomas, poet, memoirist, and Dylan Thomas's daughter, to whom the book is dedicated; to Professor Walford Davies, scholar, critic, and editor; and to my brother, Bill Nathan, author and Gower-dweller (who also checked the length of Rhossilli beach), who all read the original typescript with loving care and made valuable criticisms, corrections, and suggestions.

I am indebted to the staff of Birkbeck College library, the University of London library, and the Brompton Road and

Hornton Street libraries of the Royal Borough of Kensington and Chelsea.

A word about what kind of book this is not, and is. It is not a general introduction to the work of Dylan Thomas, nor a comprehensive critical study covering the entirety of his work. I have said a little about his drama, screenplays, and broadcasts, but concentrated on a close reading of certain poems and stories, in a personally congenial selection which I hope is representative of Thomas's work and those qualities of his imaginative achievement which I want to emphasize.

Thomas is a poet who wrote a number of outstanding poems which I judge to be great poems, using an old-fashioned adjective in an old-fashioned act of praise, and I have discussed— with others—all these poems, some of which he called "big," and some his "long exhausters," in detail, and from different points of view. They are among his most lucid poems. Dylan Thomas is an obscure and difficult poet, like other great modernists, but this is not a book in which I am particularly interested in adding to the mass of explication and exegesis which constitutes a large part of Thomas scholarship, though of course in most cases an attempted explanation, or partial interpretation, necessarily emerges from the analysis of the poem's language. I am primarily concerned to say something about Thomas's imagination, as it shows itself in his original, individual, and also rootedly traditional, language, and in the uses to which that language is put, in the several genres in which he excelled, but especially in poetry and short fiction.

In praising his poetic *oeuvre,* but also the prose narratives, particularly in *Portrait of the Artist as a Young Dog,* which I think has been neglected and undervalued, I want to contemplate his high intelligence, which has sometimes been underestimated or patronized, and which shows itself not only in his intricate craft, but in his articulation—usually implicit—of an aesthetic psychology, a humane reflexivity, and what it now seems appropriate to call the green philosophy, a politics of natural vision and a belief in what Coleridge called the unity of being, which have come to seem more familiar and more rational than they did half a century ago. Dylan Thomas is a Welsh poet who writes about people and places in Wales, so he is often, not surprisingly, discussed as a poet of region or nation, but his imagination is too large and deep for nationalism, as it is also too large and deep for anthropocentricity.

List of Abbreviations

CL   *Dylan Thomas, The Collected Letters,* ed. Paul Ferris. London: J. M. Dent, 1985.

CP   *Dylan Thomas, The Collected Poems, 1934–1953,* ed. Walford Davies and Ralph Maud. London: J. M. Dent, 1996.

CP52   *Dylan Thomas: Collected Poems, 1934–1952.* London: J. M. Dent, 1952.

CS   *Dylan Thomas: The Collected Stories.* London: J. M. Dent, 1983.

EPW   *Early Prose Writings,* ed. Walford Davies. London: J. M. Dent, 1971.

FS   *Dylan Thomas: The Filmscripts,* ed. John Ackerman. London: J. M. Dent, 1995.

JA   *A Dylan Thomas Companion,* by John Ackerman. Basingstoke and London: Macmillan, 1991.

NP   *Dylan Thomas: The Notebook Poems, 1930–1934,* ed. Ralph Maud. London: J. M. Dent, 1989.

PAYD   *Portrait of the Artist as a Young Dog,* by Dylan Thomas. Introduced by Aeronwy Thomas. London: Everyman, J. M. Dent, 1993.

QEOM *Quite Early One Morning,* ed. Aneirin Talfan Davies. London: J. M. Dent, 1954.

TB   *Dylan Thomas: The Broadcasts,* ed. Ralph Maud. London: J. M. Dent, 1991.

TP   *Dylan Thomas: The Poems,* ed. Daniel Jones. London: J. M. Dent, 1971.

TR   *Dylan Thomas: Dog among the Fairies,* by Henry Treece, London: Ernest Benn, 1947. Rev. 1956.

UMW   *Under Milk Wood,* ed. Daniel Jones. London: J. M. Dent, 1954. Rev. ed. 1974.

Unless otherwise stated, references for the poems are to CP and for the stories to PAYD.

Dylan Thomas

1. The Regional Poet

In a Europe, and on a planet, where in spite of all the internationalist movements and efforts of our century, nationalism has become a renewed threat to peace and community and social justice, Dylan Thomas has become politically important in a way he probably did not anticipate. I believe that importance rests on his total lack of nationalism, his distinctive regionalism, and his poetry of nature.

He is one of the most interesting regional poets of this century, and his Welshness—the taken-for-granted Welshness of his poetry, the more assertive Welshness of his prose, and the hard-to-define Welshness of his basic attitudes and thoughts and utterances—is admirably unmilitant, antinationalist, unpartisan, humorous, and pacifist. He was an untheoretical Socialist, but though his social compassion takes shape in the stories and occasionally in the poems, he wrote poetry which is not only unpolitical—though I think all art is, *au fond*, political—but which fascinatingly and freshly reimagines region, abstracting and metonymizing the subjects of nest and habitat while warmly sustaining the common sense of beloved times and places.

Given one of the commonest of Welsh surnames, Thomas, and what was one of the rarest Welsh or English Christian names, Dylan, that of a yellow-haired sea-loving child in that matrix of Welsh folktale and legend, *Mabinogion*, Dylan Thomas is a cradle Welsh poet. He is a non–Welsh speaker, loving Wales on the right side of idolatry, always seeming at ease with his Welshness, relaxed in a deep sense of region and regional continuity, strengthened and protected by humor, irony, and intelligence. He once described himself as restless, wanting to move from place to place, but unlike the most famous self-exiled Celtic writer of the century, James Joyce, Thomas found it necessary to wander far away but also to come back home, constantly, to a couple of places in Wales where he did most of his work.

There are absolutely no traces in Thomas's work of national pride, nor of its dangerous familiars, political self-deprecation, national defensiveness and defense. But a rooted knowledge and decently unexclusive love of the people and places of his birthplace and growth are prominent in his poetry, drama, and narrative prose. The Welshness of his writing varies from genre to genre. The stories are Welsh in location, subject matter and sometimes sources, dominantly mythological and fantastic in the early surreal stories which are often fragments from his projected and never finished long fiction about the imaginary Jarvis valley, familial and social in the realistic, or more realistic, stories of *Portrait of the Artist as a Young Dog*. In this volume of delicately connected comic and compassionate stories Thomas is caringly and consciously writing history, telling the story of the past and present in the depressed areas of South Wales, drawing directly on his knowledge of the poverty, dirt, waste and unemployment, from which he didn't suffer directly but which were physically present all round him as he grew up between the wars in his hometown of Swansea, its industrial environs, and the rural region of Carmarthenshire, where he visited his mother's sister in Fernhill farm.

The broadcasts are often acts of memory and nostalgia, consciously dwelling in the childhood past. (Of course a love of region is inseparable from a sense of continuity and association.) The broadcasts often strike a Welsh pose or affect a Welsh accent, but lightly and self-parodically, and so does the play for voices, *Under Milk Wood*, performed in 1953 and first published in 1954, which is sentimental, amusing, lyrical, and intense, creating a drama and a poetry of the surface which depends on a gallery of lively Welsh music-hall stereotypes—usually deepened and intensified—of a talkative, randy, morbid, musical and ironic nation.

There is a verse epistle, "New Quay," deliberately comic and flippant and posthumously published (in TP) which depends on national self-caricature, in a rather silly and schoolboyish vein. For instance, it has fun with a character called Jones the Cake, a "hymning Gooseberry" (first cousin to R. S. Thomas's randy deacon Davies in his fine harsh poem "The Minister"), presented in rude sexual conceits: "His head's in a nest where no bird lays her egg" is one of the more polite lines. The randy Welsh are everywhere in evidence, not only in chapel but lurking and larking in "the Welsh lechered / caves." This is the kind of fun and ridicule which is brilliantly lyricized and elevated by the poetry of *Milk Wood*, but in "New Quay" it is no more than the material and tone of a regionalized seaside postcard, reflecting the way English and Welsh joked and mimed things Welsh in the old politically incorrect world, picking on funny accents and idioms, chapels, knickers and all. In spite of the cheap humor there are times you can't help laughing, for instance at an ingenious dirty joke about cramped and cramping religion as the "Bethel-worm" deacon, generous at last, puts his penny in "the moist collection plate."

Thomas's ironic remarks about being Welsh in England, and English in Wales (for instance in a much-quoted "Address to a Scottish Society of Writers in Edinburgh," EPW), though true to his own experience, and to that of many other frequent border-crossers, his jokes in certain poems and *Under Milk Wood*, and his public stereotyping statements about feeling alienated by national institutions or emblems like mining valleys, Welsh costume, and Welsh language, are mere surface growths of observation and experience. They do not

go deep enough for poetry, though he sometimes deconstructs and mutates them in his best stories and, to some extent in *Under Milk Wood,* that original play for voices which I
think of as a compromise and a fascination.

He is a poet of region, not nation. His regionalism is in
no way obsessive or possessive. He uses and praises a beloved seascape and landscape which are at once very personal
and also marvelously abstracted and mythologized. He loves
and praises a very small geographical region—little patches
of South Wales, in West Glamorganshire and Carmarthenshire: Swansea and its surrounding beautiful rural peninsula,
Gower; and two even smaller places in South Carmarthenshire, his aunt's inland farm, Fernhill, and the seacoast village
of Laugharne which has become his shrine. In South Wales
he was born and grew up, and returned to live and work. Its
lovely and ugly places were the sacred nests of his early development and attachments, and the sites where he wrote.

They were also the places he wrote about, conspicuously,
continuously, variedly, and—almost—exclusively. In his stories he wrote about the seacoast and countryside but also
about the docks and streets and pubs and railway arches of
prewar Swansea. In his nature poetry—and nearly all his
poetry is nature poetry—he wrote about Welsh nature, in
tamed and wild habitats, just occasionally moving to write
about London's streets and river in some of his war poetry,
especially "A Refusal to Mourn the Death, by ire, of a Child,
in London," "Among those Killed in the Dawn Raid was a
Man Aged a Hundred" and "Ceremony after a Fire Raid," all
in the volume *Deaths and Entrances* (1946).

Dylan Thomas the poet draws from a deep well, taking
pains to keep its waters pure. The purity I am thinking about
has nothing to do with race or history, but is human and humane, though not anthropocentric. It is too deep for nation
and nationalism, even though the poet must reach out to the

universe with a gloved hand, to recall W. B. Yeats's clever antinationalist metaphor for regional attachment. National jokes and caricatures and stereotypes, amusing, ironic, and affectionate Thomas keeps for prose and for *Under Milk Wood*. The prose and the poetry have some superficial features, which may loosely be called Welsh, or even Celtic, a rush and race, speed, fluency, talkativeness, richness, decoration, music, excitement and rapture. But in poetry he moves behind and beyond Welsh surfaces and styles, most intelligently and consciously.

In a lecture on regionalism and nationalism, "The Regional Forecast,"[1] Seamus Heaney mentions—very briefly, and perhaps a touch warily—what he judges to be Dylan Thomas's complicity with Welsh stereotype:

> It struck me recently just how clear a case of marginalization Dylan Thomas now appears to be; a case of somebody who accepted the regional forecast even as he seemed to be totally involved with his own weather. His contributions to the BBC, even those delightful reminiscences like "A Child's Christmas in Wales,"—even, indeed, *Under Milk Wood*—are symptomatic of a not irreprehensible collusion with the stereotype of the voluble Taffy. His purely lyric gift was in the keeping of an intelligence insufficiently wary; indeed his was a clear case of a provincial imagination as defined by Patrick Kavanagh: always looking over its shoulder to see if the metropolis was in favor of its subjects and procedures. (p. 13)

Heaney's judgment is expressed rapidly and metaphorically: in *Under Milk Wood* and most of the broadcasts, the so-called "not irreprehensible collusion with the stereotype" is qualified by humor and irony, and seems to me neither naive nor unaware of what is happening. But whatever we think of Thomas's play with stereotypes of Welshness—and such play is serious and dangerous—neither the prose nor the drama seems to me to show any anxiety about metropolitan approval, and the poetry and some of the stories show an imaginative capacity to reach out from regional attachment to the natural world in a way it seems inappropriate to call provincial.

The political implications of the best stories go beyond the crippling depression in South Wales, where they are located and particularized. The poetry is more about the green world than about Wales. Thomas can feel, imagine, feel for feeling and imagine imagination, in a dimension where concepts of province, metropolis, and country are or become irrelevant, as I hope to show in this book.

When there is a provincial imagination in the poetry, it is presented with a sophisticated awareness and an ironic air of quotation which may be thought to permit or license reprehensible collusion but which may also be judged to shrug it off. I think the best example of such detached placing, with a humorous critical awareness of complicity and stereotype, is "After the funeral," probably also the best example of Thomas's capacity to release and control strong feeling, in this case a rapture of pity and praise.

It is his first elegy and one of his most personal and accessible poems, which he began to write early and worked on for a number of years before publishing. It is one of his big poems, not a long poem, which mythologizes personal feeling and personalizes myth, travels a considerable emotional distance in its short space, and is one of his great "long exhausters," as he called them. Not every good or praised poet writes such poems, but in this respect Thomas is in the company of John Donne, John Keats, Matthew Arnold, Yeats and W. H. Auden.

This simple and complex poem begins with a criticism of provincial Welsh mourning tongues and habits, in a harsh and grotesque caricature of Welsh funeral rites, which uses brilliant transferences and synecdoches, dramatizing insincerities then breaking them to produce the character and persona of a sincerely mourning boy. This past self of the narrator and the poet resembles and represents the little boy given a royal welcome by his aunt, Annie Jones, heroine of "The Peaches," generous and distressed hostess of Gorsehill, which was based on what he once described, in a letter to his friend Trevor Hughes, as the "insanitary" farm of Fernhill, in Carmarthenshire (CL, p. 13).

The boy is presented in the context of the mourning, praising, and weeping, all denigrated in physically specific grotesqueness:

> After the funeral, mule praises, brays,
> Windshake of sailshaped ears, muffle-toed tap
> Tap happily of one peg in the thick
> Grave's foot, blinds down the lids, the teeth in black,
> The spittled eyes, the salt ponds in the sleeves,
> Morning smack of the spade that wakes up sleep,
> Shakes a desolate boy who slits his throat
> In the dark of the coffin and sheds dry leaves.

In the letter to Hughes, Thomas describes his feelings about his dying aunt, with an apparent mixture of candor and indulgent self-consciousness, and perhaps a dash of affectation:

> She is dying. She is dead. She is alive. It is all the same thing. I shall miss her bi-annual postal orders. That's all. And yet I like—liked—her. She loves—loved—me. Am I . . . callous & nasty? Should I weep? Should I pity the old thing? For a moment, I feel I should. There must be something lacking in me. . . . It's self, self, all the time. (p. 13)

Whatever was lacking, the poet imaginatively solves the problem of reconciling past affection with present coldness by dramatizing three kinds of mourning, one merely conventional and false, one simply and unself-consciously sincere, and another more complexly mixed and imaginative than either of these. He had already written a satirical poem about funerals, inspired by Ann's death but not mentioning her, of which only one line, the first, was used, to begin the newer poem. The earlier "notebook" poem concentrates on an unpleasantly aggressive picture of the perceived hypocritical community of Welsh funeral rites, and refers with deliberate and impersonalizing coldness to "man or woman" and "him or her," with no particulars specified, except for one glance of sympathy, at "the ancient face" of the dead. He grafted the particulars of Ann's death onto the first highly generalized poem in which he kept her out (NP, p. 129), and used the false mourning—cleverly if not altogether fairly or admirably—to differentiate the true grief of the boy, whose sorrow is gently played with and exaggerated. Thomas then lets the boy grow up into the more detached and articulate narrator and poet, whose mourning is also played with and exaggerated, but more broadly and ironically, as he is allowed to lament and praise, get up, "stand" "alone," and keep a vigil "for this memorial's sake." The poem works itself up into an intense and effusive lament for the dead woman, reaching its peak of eloquence in the equivalent of the Welsh preacher's ecstatic *hwyl*, which may be spoken rhapsodically or even sung. But even here there is the guarded and ironic "snivelling," and the *hwyl* doesn't run for long:

I stand, for this memorial's sake, alone
In the snivelling hours with dead, humped Ann
Whose hooded, fountain heart once fell in puddles
Round the parched world of Wales and drowned each sun.

The abandonment to high feeling is brilliantly checked, parenthesized in an act of reflexive criticism which manages to be candid without chill or ironic self-deprecation:

(Though this for her is a monstrous image blindly
Magnified out of praise).

Thomas knew exactly what he was doing with this self-criticism, told his friend and fellow poet, Vernon Watkins (the correspondent to whom he wrote most, and most analytically, about language and craft), that he was "completely rewriting" the poem, making it longer and better, and finally explained:

> Now here is the Anne Jones poem, & now I think it is more of a poem. . . . I knew it was feeble as it stood before, & the end of it—that is the part that becomes the new brackets—was too facile &, almost, grandiosely sentimental. (By the way, when you type it, will you spell Anne as Ann: I just remember that's the right way: she was an ancient peasant aunt.) (CL, p. 288)

Ann is called only by her first name in the poem, and significantly isolated and separated from her marriage and family. Like other heroes and heroines of English elegy, Henry King in Milton's "Lycidas," for instance, or Keats in Shelley's "Adonais," she is first buried, then revived for metamorphosis and apotheosis. Like Lycidas she is not only resurrected but made into a fertility figure, a Welsh rural working-class Fisher Queen, though the grand solemnity of her figure is lightened by a joke about the "parched" Welsh weather as Dylan Thomas transforms wet South Wales into a wasteland: the epithet "parched" is a strong apt metaphor for describing a region devastated between the wars by poverty, unemployment, and economic waste.

When Stephen Spender suggested in a *Spectator* review of the *Collected Poems* that Thomas had "doubtless" been influenced by "Welsh bardic poetry,"[2] Thomas wrote to thank him for his perceptive praise, but added, "I'm not influenced by Welsh bardic poetry. I can't read Welsh" (CL, p. 855). The scholar and BBC producer Aneurin Talfan Davies, who knew the poet well, has recorded his personal knowledge of Thomas's interest in the intricacies of the famous and favored

Welsh form of *cynghanedd*.[3] Katharine Loesch, in her pamphlet *Welsh Poetic Syntax and the Poetry of Dylan Thomas*,[4] has suggested that Thomas may also have been influenced by verbless sentences and syntactical dislocations common in the mediaeval poet Dafydd ap Gwilym—like Thomas a green poet—and other later strict Welsh poets. It is very unlikely that Thomas, a poet so interested in the history of poetry, and poetry in Wales, so fascinated by alliterative and assonantal systems, so devoted to the hacking and sawing of his craft and sullen art, so close to the bardic tradition through his great uncle, William Thomas, preacher and bard, after the second part of whose bardic name, Gwilym Marles, Dylan Thomas got his second name, Marlais, should not have picked up some knowledge of the strict meters.

Like many children of his generation, Thomas was not brought up speaking Welsh, even though his parents were bilingual, but he was acquainted with Welsh speakers and Welsh scholars. In my day, a decade later, Welsh was a compulsory subject in elementary and grammar schools, but Thomas would probably not have learned it at his little private school and when he was at Swansea Grammar School Welsh was not a compulsory subject. He is said to have done no work as a Grammar-School boy but he would certainly have come into some contact with Welsh, if only in hymns and the national anthem. He would also have heard it spoken, as I did myself, accurately and inaccurately, in the streets and pubs as well as in Fernhill farm. Once or twice he quotes snippets of simple Welsh in the broadcasts, for instance in "Return Journey" (TB), and his talk on "Welsh Poetry" (TB) shows interest and knowledge.

In any case, though Welsh prosody is clearly best appreciated in Welsh poetry, it is not a closed system, but—like classical quantitative meters and medieval alliterative verse—has been imitated or adapted by a number of poets writing in English, some who knew the original language and some who did not. As any non-Welsh reader and writer can readily test, its rules are perfectly intelligible to anyone who understands the rules and conventions of English prosody, and though it is said that it takes five years to learn to use *cynghanedd*, it has been adopted by William Barnes, Hardy, Hopkins, Wilfred Owen, Graves, and other less musically proficient poets. Thomas may well have learned what he knew about Welsh prosody from Hopkins, who learned Welsh when he was in St. Beuno's, in North Wales, and was greatly inspired by Barnes and by bardic prosody; Thomas denied this influence at least once, but his practice, and some of his references to Hopkins, contradict the denial.

One of the best-known demonstrations of *cynghanedd* in Hopkins is a line from "God's Grandeur," "And wears man's smudge and shares man's smell" where the second half-line repeats the consonants *r, s, m, n, s, sm* from the first half-line. Many examples from Hopkins and Thomas are picked out by Alan Llwyd in his article "*Cynghanedd* and English Poetry." [5] Llwyd quotes a line from "Poem in October," "Though the town below lay leaved with October blood" where the internal rhyme and consonance conforms with a form of *cynghanedd* much favored by Hopkins, and used in "The Windhover," "Fall, gall themselves, and gash gold-vermilion." (The subject is much more complicated than this quick sketch suggests, since there are many forms of *cynghanedd* and they involve accent as well as consonance and assonance.)

Alan Llwyd recalls that "Rhydwen Williams, a Welsh poet, discussed *cynghanedd* . . . with Thomas, and Dylan is reported as saying: 'If I was writing in Welsh, I would write *cynghanedd.*'" [6] In "After the funeral" the repetition and reordering of *s, p, l,* and *t* in "spittled and saltponds," and *b* and *l* in "babble and bellbuoy" recall the consonant sequence of *cynghanedd* frequently found in Hopkins. This and many other lines which are certainly not strict examples of *cynghanedd* show the fine and complex effects of internally linked and crossed alliteration and assonance with internal rhyme, reminiscent rather than imitative of strict device, apt enough for that bard on the raised hearth. I have italicized letters in the following ten-, eleven-, and twelve-syllable lines—common variations on the iambic pentameter—to show the characteristic crossings, repetitions, internal half-rhymes and eye-rhymes, variations of the vowel and consonant chime, with stress-pattern accompaniment, which may have been inspired by the form, or by its many adaptations in Hopkins, and were practiced in many other poems by this poet who had a fine ear and loved playing with sound patterns:

> Win*dsha*ke of *sails*haped ear*s*, muffle-*t*oed *tap* . . .

> The *spittled* eye*s*, the *salt p*ond*s* in the *sl*eeve*s* . . .

> *Babb*le like a *bellb*uoy over the *h*ymning *h*eads. . . .

> *Fl*ood of *h*er *h*eart's *f*ame; she wou*l*d *l*ie *d*um*b* and *d*eep.

Another formal feature in this and many other poems is the caesura dividing a balanced alliteration (repeated, as above, in the second line's *s*s and *l*s, or new, as in the first and third lines, or repeated and new, as in the fourth line); but this is a dominant conventional pattern in Anglo-Saxon and Middle English—also available to Thomas in translations and textbooks—as well as in Welsh medieval poetry.

Though "After the funeral" may give special pleasure to students of Welsh prosody, it can't be said to be Thomas's most Welsh poem in its craft: "Fern Hill" and other poems show similar techniques, and many of Thomas's revisions— conveniently illustrated in editorial notes (CP) and in the notebook poems (NP)—show an incessant concern with assonantal and alliterative patterns: Thomas's metaphors of hacking, sawing, toiling, and hewing are strictly appropriate. But in the elegy for Ann Jones the soft and subtle Welsh prosodic echoes are thematic, making the poem an amusingly and touchingly local Welsh *occupatio,* as it mimics, complicates, criticizes, and remakes the conceited and extravagant styles of mourning, locally and traditionally ceremonial, in a complex form and style which are congenial to the poet. He is drawing on English traditions but bringing out, without flaunting, an appropriately elaborate Welshness for the occasion. In the intricately written sentences and sections of the poem the speaker consciously puts on the persona of a bard and cleverly invokes the grandeur of an ancient tradition to license a style which first struck the poet as grandiose and sentimental, as well as to criticize, improve, and dignify what he harshly judged the overdone, hypocritical, and lachrymose behavior at a Welsh funeral. The problems of criticizing and praising Welsh mores and his own exaggerated and rhapsodic poetry are solved at one stroke: "I, Ann's bard on a raised hearth, call all / The seas to service."

This poem rises to the heights, then revises the rising as indecorous, "she would lie dumb and deep / And need no druid." The image of druid joins that of bard, appropriately bringing in an older religion as well as an older poetry, so the poem succeeds in praising and in placing the act of praise, in various times and traditions.

Not only Celtic traditions: Ann's funeral is de-Christianized, taken out of doors, made into a pagan druidical ceremony, and the language is allowed to swell again, as birds and trees extend the apotheosis, just as the tides and oceans do for Lycidas, making him a dying god who becomes part of cyclically regenerative nature. The pagan feeling for a green world is also fully in keeping with the Celtic traditions of Welsh poetry, which would certainly have been known to Thomas, through conversation and reading translations. The great fourteenth-century poet Dafydd Ap Gwilym and the more orthodox sixteenth-century Edmund Price, Archdeacon of Merioneth, image similar ecstatic metamorphoses of Christian church into a wild green nature.

Language and feeling are splendidly released in what Hopkins in his sonnet "To R.B." calls "the roll, the rise, the carol,

the creation." Here the free-thinking poet uses a dramatization which shows and controls the *hwyl*, the rapturous release
of strong feeling expected in Welsh sermons. (He mimes and
constructs its lyrical flight as his Christian posthumous rival,
R. S. Thomas, never does, though in his poem "The Minister," he describes it.)

The poet's surrogate constructs a memorial statue for the
dead woman (most unlike Ann Jones's actual humble tomb):
a "skyward statue / With the wild breast and blessed and
giant skull," which is magnified and grand like the language
of Ann's elegy and encomium. It is a memorial, like many traditional monumental texts, which remembers the actuality
while proposing an ideal. Her working woman's old arthritic
hands, soaked and wrung by the washtub—symbol and synecdoche for a woman's hard wet work, especially on a poor
farm—are dignified in affectionate metamorphosis. Those
soapsuds become cloud lather, in the kind of brilliantly grotesque, almost comic, metaphor which allowed John Donne,
in his "Valediction: Forbidding Weeping," for instance, to
joke about lovers breathing each other's breath, in a conceit
which is weird, scientifically apt and also passionately reso-
nant and serious. The old pained hands are depicted realistically but their cramping distortion also makes a perfect image and synecdoche for that narrow and repressive fanatical
religion, twisted and twisting.

Welsh poverty and Welsh nonconformist religion are causally linked in one stroke of the poet's wit, in a characteristically subtle and playful interchange of vehicle and tenor.
Some of the features of a poor farming culture—a subject
dealt with more fully in Thomas's story "The Peaches," and
much more overtly and politically in the work of R. S.
Thomas—are indicted, with humor as well as high serious-
ness. The point of the passing comparison with the more explicit and didactic writing of R. S. Thomas is not to criticize
the more nationalistic, though no more Welsh, writer but to

emphasize the fashion in which Dylan Thomas moves intuitively away from polemic: even when he is attacking, as he is at the outset of this poem, in its origin and its retained beginning, he moves on to sympathy, here showing the other side of Welsh funeral rhetoric in his act of praise. He knows the culture so well—and is probably writing for others who know it equally well—that he does not need to spell it out, preach, generalize, or abstract an idea or ideology. He is of course adopting the preacher's stance, not only the liberating wild *hwyl*, but also what W. H. Auden in *New Year Letter* calls "the preacher's loose, immodest tone," if amusingly, ironically, critically, and self-critically. He is also, characteristically, more at home with the positive passion of love than the negative passion of anger, as the radical revision behind, and within, the poem shows.

As well as a particularized and implicit handling of the Welsh culture within the poem, there is a breadth of literary tradition behind the poem. The transformation works on the Welsh front parlor as well as the dead woman, as the typical, constricted, ornamental, hideous but still sacred objects, a stuffed fox, doubly dead, and a potted fern, ironic front room icon of green Fernhill (to be revised in "Fern Hill") are restored to a wild, free, large and fertile nature. The critique of modern Welsh funeral culture is justified, but shown to be personal, and made good, by the pastoral rites, creating a refreshed ceremony which, despite bard and druid, show Thomas's deep knowledge of the English elegiac tradition, in which versions of a vegetation ritual of resurrection, and an apotheosis, conventionally accompany encomium and lamentation, in a poetic equivalent of burial, encomium, and prayers for resurrection. Cultures cross and join. "After the funeral" is his "Lycidas," just as "Fern Hill" is his "Paradise Lost," though perhaps also is his "Paradise Regained."

Perhaps the only other equally Welsh poem is the Prologue poem he wrote for the 1952 edition of his *Collected Poems*, which was first called "Author's Prologue" (apparently by the publisher, not the poet) and then shortened to "Prologue." After struggling to meet his publisher's request for a formal prose introduction, he gave this up in favor of verse, and wrote a poem the intricacy of whose verse scheme is only outdone by its invisibility, since the long, 101-short-lined poem rhymes the first line with the last in the repetition, "now," and turns on a central couplet which is divided by a section break, and which may or may not alert the reader, unlikely to have noticed the rhyme scheme before:

Sheep white hollow farms

To Wales in my arms.

Thomas said he didn't know why he had "acrosticked" himself so, and did not wait for an answer (CL, p. 838). I think one answer is implicit in the humor of the appropriately and inappropriately strict form: it is very Welsh in its newly invented and heavily disguised strict prosody, both form and disguise a joke. It is very much more Welsh than the brief prose introductory note published in *Collected Poems* (1952):

I read somewhere of a shepherd who, when asked why he made, from within fairy rings, ritual observances to the moon to protect his flocks, replied: "I'd be a damn' fool if I didn't!" These poems, with all their crudities, doubts and confusions, are written for the love of Man and in praise of God, and I'd be a damn' fool if they weren't.

My reason for finding this comment sentimental is the knowledge that Thomas's poetry is about much more than the capitalized "God" and "Man" of this credo. Here he seems to be affecting simplicity and selling his vision short. The assumption or adoption of pastoral magic is inadequate for a poet whose work does not make high claims to humanism or theism, only a modest and quiet obeisance to natural unity, which is sometimes not altogether happily called pantheism. It uses religious metaphor of several kinds, but need not be, or be derived from, any kind of theology.

"Prologue" uses a couple of familiar and assimilated Welsh words, "*bryn*" —hill—familiarized for non–Welsh speakers in thousands of names, of hills and houses, and the short form of the common contraction of David, "*Dai*" in "Dai Mouse." He remythologizes the Deluge, lightly and comically relocating it in Wales, and just at the poem's central rhyme junction it streams across the "Sheep white hollow farms"— after a space in the middle of the sentence—"to Wales in my arms," when the reader can begin to read both form and allegory. The ambiguous grammar makes the flood stream to Wales in the speaker's arms, and makes Wales lie within their protective hold. Towards the end ark-builder and creatures and all will ride "Under the stars of Wales." The animals are Welsh, of course, the rooks fondly and comically "dark Welsh and reverent," like ministers of religion.

One of Thomas's critics, John Ackerman, insists that the poem must be seen as a genuine prologue to the poetry (JA, p. 51), and it is true that of all his self-referential poems this one is most explicit about the range and subject-matter of an *oeuvre.* The poet is explicitly present, casting himself as a new Noah, another man acquainted with the deep waters, another builder (of verse), another dweller in a flimsy wooden house, and also another drunk, "Drinking Noah of the bay," with a light wry transatlantic touch in the treble meaning of that "moonshine / Drinking."

The seat of imagination, often present in his poems, is his actual working shed in Laugharne, rickety and wooden, and on the cliff overlooking the sea, if not in the sea, "my sea-shaken house." But the real ark is his work, "my bellowing ark," the collected poems, larger than life, shouted out in a loud voice, much worked on, and containing a bestiary, here localized as ringdove, gulls, pipers, cockles, crows, geese, curlew, heron, salmon, owl, hare, fox and mouse. Of course most of these air and sea creatures, literally unendangered by flood, don't need Noah's ark, but Dylan Thomas's imaginary ark guarantees them a kind of imaginative survival. Not one of the great poems, I think, but it has its own lighthearted charm and fun. The location in Wales is delicately and delightfully touched, a conceit not to be taken too seriously, but no mere joke either:

> We shall ride out alone, and then,
> Under the stars of Wales,
> Cry, Multitudes of arks! Across
> The water lidded lands,
> Manned with their loves they'll move,
> Like wooden islands, hill to hill.

After that enthusiastic proliferation of arks, we have not only the biblical dove but a merrily hailed miscellany, including a fox and an English-named Tomtit joined by the Welsh "Dai mouse." The poem does not end with a rainbow, but with a blossoming: "The flood flowers now." This is a new deluge, seawater that goes on flowing, destruction which does not end in a promise of no more destruction, and a refuge in the arks of art, which do not land on an Ararat but go on sailing and weathering a flood which never does dry up, at least not in imaginable time.

Ackerman suggests that Thomas conflates Noah with a famous mythological drunken Welshman, Seithenyn, "whose drunken negligence led to the flooding of the lowlands" (Cantre'r Gwaelod) "now Cardigan Bay." Whether this is a subtext in the poem or not, the flood is a good local image for the actual tide, and Noah, flood, and ark are perfect for Thomas's comic but serious ceremony of poetic affirmation. The echo "now" in first and last lines is compounded by similar repetitions ("sun" and "end") of the second and third lines and the last but one and last but two, and, once noticed, makes a good neat clinching beginning, connection, and conclusion. The poem is set in Wales, and has a Welsh subject, but the deep subject is the natural world, which only happens to be Welsh, not uniquely the matter of Wales. The prologue poem appropriately celebrates the deep subject of a unity of being, lightheartedly and unportentously. Like "After the funeral," the poem is both very Welsh and much more than Welsh, assuming a Welsh costume only in order to cast it off as superficial.

The same is true of other poems with even more clearly named and designated Welsh locations. Another seascape poem, and another poem that can be visited, like "Prologue" and "Fern Hill," is "Over Sir John's Hill," which contains the specified Laugharne landscape of hill, estuary and sea, and has its key place-name, which is local but also suggests the prevailing figure of personification and the theme of judgment, in which the poet revises his Welsh character by rechristening himself young Aesop. The local landscape is realized, but also made grotesque and strange as the poem's playful imposition of fable on a familiar landscape celebrates and explicates the place-name, but in a way which insists upon the arbitrariness, almost the inappropriateness, of writing about nature in a religious and forensic moral allegory. The poem abstracts locality, to concentrate on the relationship of the natural world and the language in which poets write about that natural world. Wales provides an occasion and an example, though drawing on a close and loving knowledge of a place, its shapes, scenes, and animal life.

The Cwmdonkin Park poem, "The hunchback in the park," though alive with the poet's sacred characters, places, and objects—which have been posthumously joined by some new Dylan Thomas touristic features, all eminently visitable—is a poem about the solitude, play, and poverty of life in parks, and about creativity. Though an actual remembered place is re-created, it could really be anywhere, and the poem is certainly not appropriately or adequately described as a Welsh poem about a Welsh place. It was once incorporated in a radio talk, "Reminiscences of Childhood" (TB) and then given a name, context, and extended discussion, but as a lyric, published in isolation, it is about any park, a public space which is a playground for happy children and a refuge for lonely people and down-and-outs.

It locates its action and feeling in a sacred region, but it is a less regionally conscious poem than "Sir John's Hill," which locates action and feeling in a named and specific beloved place, while consciously converting or assimilating that feeling to the larger themes of art and nature. As the hill (Sir John's) and the river ("fishing in the tear of the Towy") are named, there is a special act of affectionate and proprietorial preservation and memorial, the kind of ritual signified and elaborated, for instance, in Wordsworth's "Poems on the Naming of Places" which perform an act of christening, or rechristening, dwelling on a beloved spot and showing the awareness of the very act of so dwelling. "Dwelling" indeed speaks for itself as an apt metaphor for such loving poetry of place, and describes what happens, or seems to happen, in many of Thomas's best poems about the natural world, recalling it, evaluating it, and revisiting it, with fondness but no sentimentality. He called Swansea, his "ugly, lovely town," "the most romantic town I know" (TB, p. 222) though he is capable of writing about it unromantically. But "The hunchback in the park" recalls and concentrates on people, and the place is only significant as a populated territory and playground.

To return to Welshness. As we come to know them, the poems and stories may be read as a whole, creating our sense of the *oeuvre* or body of work, and gradually the places and things accumulate or cohere to create a sense of place. There is a Swansea-Gower-Fernhill-Laugharne matrix or image bank, containing local places, hills, features, buildings and objects, schools, the new asylum, streets, shops, docks, railway arches, bays and headlands, and this is drawn on for different purposes and with different emotional and thematic emphases.

The park details belong to this matrix. In "The hunchback in the park," the remembered boy who sailed his ship in the fountain basin, played games in the groves, and no doubt joined in making fun of the hunchback, is a character who acts as the medium, and though he is essential to the poem, the incarnated character of the hunchback, a real man imagined and remembered, comes to occupy the center of the poem, to displace the boy and the place which brings them together.

Cwmdonkin Park, a stone's throw from Thomas's birthplace and childhood home in Cwmdonkin Drive, and partly visible from the house, crops up in other poems and some of the stories. It is present, for instance, in a poem about writing, and perhaps about a change in writing and imaginative direction, "Once it was the color of saying," where a park is a view, and a source of imagery. Its gate, drinking fountain, bell, groves, benches, rockery, railings and willows are specific and also general, salient features of a park which are not especially Welsh. The park in the park poem is not called Cwmdonkin, and some of its features—the old ones, because it has been greatly changed, not only by a Thomas water garden and memorial stone, but by the obliteration of the reservoir by a German bomb—a dahlia garden and the cricket pitch, are not mentioned. (They are mentioned in two of the broadcast talks.)

The reservoir was bombed, but though he lamented the famous and destructive bombing of Swansea, Thomas wrote his blitz poems about deaths and destructions in London, not Swansea. As he refuses to mourn the death of a child in his great war poem "A Refusal to Mourn the Death, by Fire, of a Child in London," he dignifies the London region of "the riding Thames," but interestingly incorporates the common name of a Welsh chapel, "the round Zion." (It doesn't have to be Welsh, of course, but there were lots of Zions and Seions around in South Wales in his day, and one Mount Zion at the top of Cradock Street in Swansea, which was damaged in the blitz.)

Welsh places are named and sometimes specified in the stories and broadcasts, but though they are points on a visitor's map, now that Thomas has become a tourist attraction, they are not like Yeats's named places, Innisfree, Lissadell, Glendalough, Lugnagall and Ben Bulben, whose mellifluous Irishness sometimes overwhelms geography, as in the mistily located Innisfree, and the inaccurately used Lugnagall. Thomas doesn't do much with the exotic music of Welsh names, apart from the rivers Tawe and Towy, and Llareggyb's river "Dewi." Indeed, he does not create the poetry of place by the naming of places, and the very absence of Welsh place-names diminishes or banishes the national feeling, even the regional feeling. ("The Hunchback of Cwmdonkin" would have been a different poem from the one we have, I imagine.) It's interesting that the poem with a place-name title has an English place-name, that of Sir John, though it contains a Welsh river, the Towy. His most famous place-name, "Llareggyb," is a rude playful joke about Welsh place-names. "Fern Hill" is an English name, though of a Welsh place, which may look like an exception, but the title carefully and pointedly breaks down the actual place-name, "Fernhill," into its component, to re-create a place and time, analyzing the word to spell out and specify a larger and wilder greenness. More stories than poems use actual Welsh names, though only once in the title, "Where Tawe flows," which is a playfully ironic lyrical label for a comic celebration of a group of Swansea aspirant writers, including "Mr. Thomas." Thomas wrote self-consciously and jokily to Pamela Hansford Johnson about Welsh place-names, but not always sincerely, as when he said some names were as unintelligible to him as to her, Pwlldu, for instance, which in spite of its difficult "ll"—not avoided in the radio talk "Return Journey" (TB)—was a familiar place-name in Swansea. You don't even have to have Welsh-speaking parents, as Thomas did, to be able to pronounce the local place-names accurately.

In the stories he occasionally uses Welsh slang words, but only ones commonly used by non-Welsh speakers, and anglicizing them, like "*toop*" ("*twp*": daft) and "*Diu*" (*Duw*: God). He carefully researched Welsh poets and poets who visited Swansea, for an article in the school magazine, and his attitude to the Welsh language which he didn't know seems to have been honest and dignified. (For instance, even when he makes rude jokes about the land of his fathers, he never uses the word "Taffy," in my experience used more by people who aren't Welsh than by the Welsh themselves, which Heaney mentioned as an example of stereotype in the comment quoted earlier.) The small sprinkling of Welsh words cannot be seen as an affectation, but some of his show-off deprecating remarks to Pamela Hansford Johnson almost certainly were, and also perhaps suggest an unease or guilt—to my knowledge felt by other monolingual Welsh children, brought up bilingual parents. Moreover, the deprecation was clearly entangled with his longings—like Joyce's, though expressed much less poetically, dramatically and traumatically—to fly the nets of family, country, and religion. He did fly them, but only temporarily, and though he needed the stimulus and opportunities of London culture, it was to Wales he returned, and in Wales, as his critics and friends have always insisted, that he did nearly all his work as a writer.

In some of his finest poems, for instance, "The force that through the green fuse" and the later poems written for his own birthdays, "Fern Hill," and "In Country Sleep," the Welsh landscape and the Welsh memories are even more abstracted than in the firmly located but deeply generalized

"Sir John's Hill." In "Fern Hill," a romantic celebration of what Wordsworth called the holiness of the heart's affections, Thomas playfully gilds the real farm and the real childhood with a radiance that reconstructs and repopulates Milton's story of Creation. The poem knows that it is Welsh in one turn of phrase, the rare example in Thomas of a common Welsh conjunction intensifier, "Lovely and watery," appropriate in the remaking of a childhood's colloquial language. But the known and familiar landscape of the place where Thomas spent holidays with his uncle and aunt is metamorphosed, and a region is used for more than a regional poetry.

Similarly, "Poem in October" uses a primal scene of childhood and landscape but in a way which is only incidentally and implicitly Welsh:

And I saw in the turning so clearly a child's
Forgotten mornings when he walked with his mother
    Through the parables
      Of sun light
  And the legends of the green chapels

  And the twice told fields of infancy
That his tears burned my cheeks and his heart moved in
    mine.
  These were the woods the river and sea
    Where a boy
    In the listening
Summertime of the dead whispered the truth of his joy
To the trees and the stones and the fish in the tide.
    And the mystery
      Sang alive
  Still in the water and singingbirds.

The fields of infancy were richly free, wild, and truly pastoral, and naturally nourished the child's spontaneous animism. The religious and local imagery in the parables of sun and light, and the green chapels, are signifiers of a natural religion, and the Bible fables and chapel, as in "After the funeral," are extended far beyond institution and region. Region is freed, opened, and remythologized.

The act of remythologizing clearly puts us in touch with the level below conscious recall at which such continuities are created by a Wordsworthian natural piety, vision, and re-creation. The vital child isn't just a little Welsh boy with his Welsh mother having a very good time listening to her stories—though he once was—but also an ecstatic mouthpiece for the poet as he plumbs the source and origin of creativity. This is childhood intuition, play, ease, and also love.

The child is an image of the artist, recalled as an imaginative singer as well as a listener. The subjects of continuity and stability so important in all our developments and here given a brilliantly fresh local color, are intricated, expanded, and elucidated, by the paradox of remembering a forgotten past:

And I saw in the turning so clearly a child's
Forgotten mornings . . .

Region must be remembered and forgotten.

I want to add a personal postscript. I happen to share Dylan Thomas's South Welsh region, like him being born, a decade later, in Swansea, like him living close to Cwmdonkin Park, five minutes away from his home in Cwmdonkin Drive, possessing Swansea's parks and the Gower peninsula as a childhood and adolescent playground, experiencing Swansea's poverty and depression in the late twenties and thirties, knowing its chapels, its grassroots Socialism, its air raids, its streets, shops, schools, and public buildings, some destroyed and some surviving. I shared most aspects of the upper-working-class or lower-middle-class culture, though not the privileges and dangers of the Welsh rearing and bonding of young males. I do not want to write about Thomas's poetry of region without mentioning my own involvement, as I might not be writing about his work if I hadn't been born in South Wales, or if I were, would be writing about it differently.

Brought up on English romantic poetry and the Georgians, I was dazzled and puzzled on first looking into Dylan Thomas. (I never met him but must sometimes have passed him in the streets.) He was my first modernist, and I first heard of him in Pwlldu, a smuggler's bay in South Gower, one of Thomas's so-called unpronounceable places which he doesn't put into a story. I was visiting relations who were camping on a high cliff overlooking the sea and storm beach. My uncle, Walter Incledon, chapel organist, book collector, autodidact, and family intellectual, came out of a tent, handed me a magazine, and said in his customary dry tone, "Have you read this new poet they're all making a fuss about?" I can't recall a poem or a line or a word, only my first impressions, no doubt fictionalized and distorted over the years, of bright strange imagery, strongly attractive but obscure. I don't know exactly when that was, probably just before the war began, in the late thirties. Then and later, I responded with interest and a decidedly incomplete understanding, as recommended by Coleridge and T. S. Eliot.

A year or two later I came across a copy of Roger Roughton's surrealist magazine *Contemporary Poetry and Prose* (July 1936) on a secondhand bookstall in Swansea market, a Victorian glass building shattered in the blitz, and rebuilt. Two sonnets by Thomas, "From the oracular archives and the parchment" and "Let the talè's sailor from a Christian voyage," paired as "Two Poems Towards a Poem" kept congenial company with Wallace Stevens, E. E. Cummings (his name in upper case), and Isaac Babel. Though I found all the contributions exceptionally obscure, I began to recognize a genre, and to enjoy the dislocations and fantasy. My favorite was a poem by the editor called "Soluble Noughts and Crosses; or, California, Here I Come," which began "In a small theodolite of paper / I could see the eyelash of a girl." Thomas's contributions were later published, with two small changes in hyphenation, in *Twenty-five Poems,* as poems IX and X, concluding the obscure and much-discussed sonnet sequence "Altarwise by owl-light." It was my first taste of his morbid sexuality, and of the green world savored in one of his splendid similes, "Green as beginning."

When I began to teach, I occasionally lectured on Dylan Thomas and remember taking a practical criticism class on "The force that through the green fuse drives the flower," and admitting that I didn't understand everything in the poem. I read the poems aloud with great pleasure, and it was many years before I was told by Wynn Thomas of the University College of Swansea, that when Welsh men read them aloud they tended to model themselves on Thomas, whereas Welsh women were freed from that imperative.

I began by pronouncing his name "Dullan" not "Dillon," as everyone in Swansea did, and some still do. He told Pamela Hansford Johnson that it was "Dillon" but there are still arguments about this, and "Dullan" was certainly what came naturally in the forties, and was the pronunciation used by people who knew him, like his close friend Fred Janes's sister, Kitty Jones, who amazed us by telling how Dylan used to eat chrysanthemums. In London everyone said "Dillon" and one day I heard myself saying it too, without ever making a conscious decision about it.

I was not one of the critics who admired him without reservation, and still dislike the melodramatic flourish and stridency in some poems, for instance "The hand that signed the paper," and "And death shall have no dominion," and the schoolboyish humor, morbid sexuality, and the double entendres of some puns and wisecracks, which I was secretly thrilled by on first reading. (Some of my criticisms were made forcibly and amusingly by Thomas himself, as I found when his letters were published.)

I have changed my mind, about what once seemed to me his sentimentality, especially in *Under Milk Wood,* a play which I seriously underestimated. Made uneasy by F. R. Leavis and my own doubts, which were in many ways bound up with my ambivalent feelings about leaving and loving Wales, reacting against local fans who seemed to romanticize Thomas because he was Welsh, but approving his own rational and humane freedom from nationalism, I decided to stop teaching him. But I went on reading. In 1973, when asked to write about him for a special Dylan Thomas number of *Poetry Wales,* I tried to decide what it was I both admired and distrusted. I reprinted the essay in my book *The Advantage of Lyric,*[7] and over the years, I've gone on teaching his work, and writing about it, and though I still have a few reservations about some of the poetry and early prose, in the end admiration has won.

The common region helped as well as hindered. I too disliked the cramped and cramping religion, and the black deacons, I too was a non–Welsh speaker (though I learned Welsh in primary and secondary school for several years). I too was English in Wales and Welsh in England. I too went to elocution lessons and developed a cut-glass accent. I too loved the cliffs and sea and sand and had sacred places and objects in Cwmdonkin Park, where my mother first took my brother and me on summer evenings, and I too lived "up the Uplands." Later, I too was an Anglo-Welsh reader of Welsh poetry in translation, acquainted with the strict meters at second hand. In England it was taken for granted that I was interested in Dylan Thomas: when I went for my first job interview I was asked about him. I lectured at the Dylan Thomas Summer School, first in Swansea, run by Thomas Thomas and Wyndham Griffiths, later in Aberystwyth, run by Walford Davies.

Sharing a region and an Anglo-Welsh culture has motivated my interest in Thomas, and sharpened my response to the form of poems, but on the whole I don't think knowing the places and objects brings me closer to individual writings. Occasionally it helps. For instance, there is one example of a puzzle which won't exist for people who don't know the Gower coast, and which is a footnote, rather than a necessary gloss, to the story "Extraordinary Little Cough." The school-boys in the story are camping at Mewslade, a small bay to the east of Rhossilli Bay, but when Little Cough (the schoolboy nickname for George Hooping) is said to perform his marathon run along the five-mile Rhossilli beach, there is no suggestion that he actually would have had to do an even longer trek, either doubling the beach run to get back, or doing a long cliff walk to or from the beach. Thomas is either not imagining the run very carefully, or may have forgotten what would be involved.

There is one other example where local knowledge may have affected my response, in this case increasing my pleasure in a work. At the end of one of Thomas's finest stories, "Who Do You Wish Was With Us?" there is a reference to what happens on the Worm (Old Norse *otmh* and Anglo-Saxon *wyrm*) or Worm's Head, a jutting tidal island, and sea serpent–shaped headland in Rhossilli Bay, Gower. The narrator and his friend cross to the headland at low tide, walk to the point, and will have to stay the night (after the story's end) because the tide has covered the causeway. The story ends with their realization that they are cut off till low water, though the detail of the marooning is withheld. In December 1933, in a long autobiographical letter to Pamela Hansford Johnson (CL, p. 62) Thomas describes how the strange isolated "seaworm of rock pointing into the channel" at the "furthest point of Gower" made him feel "like something out of the Tales of Mystery and Imagination," and relates how he was once, like his characters, accidentally marooned on the "promontory of depression." As I explain and illustrate in chapter 3, some of the descriptions of the Worm are precise, but not completely or elaborately particularized and mapped, and I think the full implications of the conclusion depend on a knowledge not spelled out in the story. At least, there are details of the action and the symbolism in the story which are better grasped if you know both the danger and the difficulty of getting to the end of the headland. The solitude, wildness, and extremity of the place are presented in the story, though the writer leaves out some aspects described in the letter just quoted, but there is one aspect of the conclusion which only someone familiar with the scene can appreciate. When we are told, in a description of an intense and ecstatic experience, that the young men are at the end of the peninsula, the native reader, familiar with the site and the map, is sharply aware that the bay of Rhossilli is at its extreme western point, the headland protruding into the sea with the northern coastline bending sharply back. The sense of extremity and isolation is stated eloquently, but the geographical detail is not completely visualized. Rhossilli and its great rock work symbolically like the county of Galway on the wild west coast of Ireland in James Joyce's story "The Dead." Saturated in his experience of the place, Thomas makes this one significant aspect—the sense of isolated westerliness—for granted, and does not dwell on it. I am not criticizing the story for a failure in particularity: if we know the scene, something is added, but as I shall show when I discuss the story in detail, in chapter 3, so much is going on in the complexly moving and self-analyzing conclusion that it doesn't matter if this one local allusion and resonance is missed by many readers. ·

2. The Modernist Poet

The Stream that is Flowing All Ways

A profound and integral artistic self-consciousness is one of the features which link Dylan Thomas with the other writers who have been more celebrated as modernists, T. S. Eliot, Joyce, Lawrence, and Woolf. Thomas is with the great radical revolutionary modernists in his innovations and his subversions, of form and style, especially in his poetry.

He is writing some time after the early poems of T. S. Eliot, especially "Preludes" and *The Waste Land,* those models of fragmentariness, dislocation, discontinuity, opacity and openness; and after Eliot's famous pronouncement in *The Dial,* "instead of narrative method, we may now use the mythical method."[1] He is writing after the transformation of *Stephen Hero*'s linear continuities and narrative fullness into the lyrical form of *A Portrait of the Artist as a Young Man* and the even less realistic and narratively complete forms of *Ulysses* and *Finnegans Wake.* He is writing after Woolf began counting the atoms as they fall on the mind and created her versions of the Joycean elastic form. He is writing after cubism's dismemberments and angularities, and the beginnings of nonfigurative art, the dislocations of mixed forms, the self-styled dilapidations of surrealism.

Compared with these more theoretical seniors, when Thomas writes conceptually about his poetry, he tends to sound old-fashioned. Perhaps he was entangled, as George Eliot reminds us we all are, in metaphor. Perhaps his art was ahead of his aesthetics. When he writes to Henry Treece about trying to "make that momentary peace which is a poem" (CL, p. 282), he is concerned with destruction and contradiction, but in the end restricted by ideas of completion and teleology: "Out of the inevitable conflict of images — inevitable, because of the creative, recreative, destructive and contradictory nature of the motivating centre, the womb of war" (CL, p. 282), and "I believe in the single thread of action through a poem, but that is an intellectual thing aimed at lucidity through narrative" (CL, p. 281), and in "Answer to an Enquiry" writing of the "individual struggle from the darkness toward some measure of light" (EPW). Such comments are hard to reconcile with the more interesting and novel suggestion, also made to Treece, that his poems are not organized round a center, and with the wonderful antisequential image of "the stream that is flowing all ways" (CL, p. 282). His remarks are sometimes contradictory, and when he explains to Treece that he is trying to elucidate but feels "it's necessarily vague to me" (CL, p. 281), he's right. When he seems to be speaking of disruption as congenial, for instance, he is both vague and obscure, as when he insists on the narrative element in poetry on the grounds that the reader needs to be given narrative to seduce or distract him while the "essence" of the poem does its work ("Answer to an Enquiry," EPW). (The introduction of "essence" here is not helpful, and the difference between his and T. S. Eliot's well-known discussion of the same idea is significant. Thomas is not at home in academic discourse.)

Thomas's critics, on fire with speculation like Jane Austen's Emma, have been keen on explication of meanings, and have sometimes tried to explain his obscurity and strangeness rather than accept and place them in the modernist tradition. They have indeed, as Loesch points out,[2] often filled in gaps which he leaves, or completed what he leaves incomplete, reading themes and patterns of a traditionally developmental and close form into his radical disruptions.

Thomas's critics have also sometimes been reluctant to

recognize, let alone praise, his modernism. George Thomas, for instance, in his article "Dylan Thomas and Some Early Readers" in *Poetry Wales*, says his early readers had "been accustomed to take a great deal of obscurity along with their entertainment,"[3] which is a recognition of the literary and cultural context, but a backhanded compliment to the modern tradition.

But at times Thomas was speaking as a modernist. When he told Treece, in the letter already quoted, that the center of his poems was "a host of images" related to each other by oppositions, and used the metaphor, native to his mind's method, of "a watertight section of the stream that is flowing all ways" (CL, p. 282), he seems to be giving his own somewhat confused version of those other more illustrious modernist metaphors of dislocation, dilapidation, and fracture, found for instance in Woolf and Lawrence, and like them voicing a new opposition to ideals and models of unity and teleology. (Later critical theory caught up with all this, resisting and attacking the New Critical habit of seeking symbolic and thematic and metaphorical unity.)

There is dislocation and radical new construction in Thomas, but many—probably most—of his poems are unified in a common and classical way, and proceed to some kind of telos or conclusion. Nearly all the poems I have already discussed have been of this kind, and many of them mount very conspicuously—sometimes erotically—to a climax which often coincides with conclusion. This is true of "If my head hurt a hair's foot," "The force that through the green fuse," "After the funeral," "The hunchback in the park," "Fern Hill," "Sir John's Hill," the birthday poems, "A Refusal to Mourn" and "Love in the Asylum."

But what marks many of the poems which do have an apparently or superficially conventional temporal form—at least a beginning and end—is a repetitiveness or suspension, a dislocation or refusal to proceed during the poem, the beginning and middle of which behave as beginnings and endings customarily do. Indeed, Thomas's beginnings and endings are often very strong, and he loves to compound them, as Shakespeare and Joyce do, beginning and ending by admitting several categories of beginning and ending.

Within the frame of beginning and ending his structure is often undeveloped and static, an eddy not a flow. Perhaps this is another way of explaining or unpacking that remark of his about the host of images at the "center" of his poems. The word "static" won't quite do, however, because within a suspension or absence of development there may be narrative-packed or action-packed images, microstructures which are unified within themselves. In part this eddying and repetition derives from his favorite structure of juxtaposed images, and from the considerable narrative compression and assertiveness of many individual images.

In part it derives from some of the unconventional syntax to which Loesch[4] has valuably drawn attention in her study of the analogues, which she believes to be sources, in Welsh bardic poetry, for example, nominal sentences and independent nominal clauses. Many of her examples seem to be disguised but readable or possible verbal sentences, and not truly nominal, but she makes the important suggestion that the image-by-image construction common in Welsh bardic poetry is behind, and gets into, many of Thomas's structures.

The other bardic device she finds in Thomas, syntactic dislocation, is a useful and plausible paradigm, but Joyce could have been the model, and there is no need to propose that Thomas read or came to know a great deal about Welsh poetry. A prosodic device like *cynghanedd* is easy to grasp in theory, though it seems unlikely that he would have been influenced just by reading about syntactic construction, a less popular and accessible subject than the famous strict meters. But Thomas didn't need just to read about the strict meters, he could see them modeled in Barnes and Hopkins and in the same way he could observe stylistic interruption and discontinuity, and nominal sentences, in Joyce, whom he did read, and who did not follow the convention of complete verbal sentences. Like Dorothy Richardson, writing at about the same time, and Woolf, a little later, but with greater daring in dislocation than either, Joyce was imitating modes and motions of consciousness which do not have to depend on or include verbal sentences, or move in a linear or chronological or logical or regular process. And behind, and before, Joyce, there was Dickens, whose gloriously irrational talkative women, like Mrs. Nickleby and Flora Finching, may well have been models for Molly Bloom and other more conventionally educated Joycean ruminative narrators, while behind them all is Shakespeare, whose Nurse and Mistress Quickly are older revolutionary models for the modernist free stream of consciousness. Thomas knew Dickens and Shakespeare too.

To return to that image of the stream flowing all ways. Some of the strong conclusions seem too strong. At times the closure of a poem may sit oddly or unworthily in its final place, as in the end to "My hero bares his nerves": "I pull the chain, the cistern moves," and the end of "Before I knocked": "And double-crossed my mother's womb," where the exhibitionist would-be shock associations with lavatory and American slang diminish the larger resonances, and close with an emphasis on the vehicle rather than the tenor. When I first read these poems as an adolescent I found such little shocks enjoyable, like jokes which made you snigger in Sunday school. With time the disruptive wisecrack has come to seem cheap and feeble, palling as ancient shocks and jokes do. I see these conclusions as failures of control rather than radical disruptions of ending, but they may be evidence that Thomas found ending poems difficult or uncongenial.

What are often radically freestanding and nonsequential are certain individual images which seem to be, or may actually be, independent units rather than parts of a developmental process. These images may seem not to attach themselves verbally or causally to antecedent and successor but to work statically, as a repeat or a round. Stasis may seem a negative term or concept, but once we give up the idea of a place in total development, the central section, or the branching tributary images or events, may appear vital and vivid. The oxymoron of that stream flowing all ways is a more faithful description of many poems than the teleological statements about making a momentary peace or moving out of the dark toward light.

There are two related "disruptive" structural features which Thomas's poetry has in common with Eliot's and Joyce's, and which are recognizable rhetorical features of modernism. In Thomas they go together and support each other. One is a conspicuous musicalization of language, which may reinforce what I have called the stasis of the middle passage, as the poem's music asserts its own sound primacy. The other is a local assertiveness and fragmentation of imagery, the dominance of part over whole, or part independent of whole.

The music, again and always, is one of the stylistic features which is sometimes identified as a Celtic characteristic, since the theory and practice of Celtic poetry insists on sound equal to or dominant over sense. This may be true, but I think it is also clearly something Thomas learned—or was encouraged to use—by reading Joyce. Although Thomas's rhythms, for instance, are strong and arresting, such strength and arrest can be found in many earlier poets—Byron and Tennyson, for example—but the aspect of musicalization which Thomas's poetry has in common with Joyce's prose is its prominent fluidity, its urge to blur the edge or boundary between word and word, phrase and phrase, sentence and sentence. When reading Thomas the ear can often be delighted and enchanted before the mind takes in the meanings, and not, I think, just because of his powerfully marked rhythms but also because the sound flow sweeps us on, language aspiring to the condition of music.

The poetic flow breaks down the fixity and definiteness of the word, setting the word itself against the word, not polemically and collisively, as in Richard II's sense, but working rather to increase the unity and smoothness of the language units in relation to each other. Words run into each other. They do so in the rush and race of "The force that through the green fuse drives the flower / Drives my green age," whose alliterative and assonantal blend enacts or mimes the event it narrates. The fluency is felt in the prolonged sentence structures of "Prologue," whose short two-beat lines make an amusingly assertive and quick-running medium for the new Welsh word-deluge. It is there in the asyndeton and rove-over lines of "Fern Hill," where childhood vitality and summer glow are merged in a pun-made dance—"the hay"—of memory as it recaptures childhood bliss:

> All the sun long it was running, it was lovely, the hay
> Fields high as the house, the tunes from the chimneys, it
>   was air
> And playing, lovely and watery.

It is there in the fast movement and flow of the far from set in concrete shape-poems which compose "Vision and Prayer," less a sequence than a series of stanzas, since not only the meaning but the last line of a poem or part sometimes runs on the first line of the next. However arbitrary, tight, limited and typographically determined the visual diamond or hourglass of these poems, or a parts of a sequence poem, appears to the eye, the movement of the language, in phrase and sentence, is extremely fluid, and since the linked poems are very short, each one achieves speed and compression, making an impression of instantaneity. Joyce and Virginia Woolf played with problems and paradoxes of narrated and narrative time, Joyce writing poetic novels which compressed time into Bloom's day and Finnegan's night, Woolf compressing Mrs. Dalloway's day and drawing out Orlando's centuries. Within their experiments they drew out narrated experience, counting the atoms, in Woolf's image, as they fell upon the mind, to dwell, or try to dwell, or show that it is impossible to dwell, on the moment, that mysterious and un-realizable time experience we cannot catch, let alone record or invent. Thomas does something similar with time play, in order to record the timeless feeling of vision and prayer in the diamond-shaped "Vision and Prayer," which is arguably his most traditional Christian poem, in a traditional form, most famously used by George Herbert in his poetry of reli-gious meditation:

Who

Are you

Who is born

In the next room

So loud to my own

That I can hear the womb

Opening and the dark run

Over the ghost and the dropped son

Behind the wall thin as a wren's bone?

In the birth bloody room unknown

To the burn and turn of time

And the heart print of man

Bows no baptism

But dark alone

Blessing on

The wild

Child.

Here is the characteristic first poem from the sequence, and a characteristically seized moment, imagined as a moment of vision, though divided into two fast movements of question and response. It emerges as a vision of strange quick birth, unlike that slow hard labor imagined for the "ordinary" child in "If my head hurt a hair's foot." Each poem in the two-sectioned, twelve-poemed "Vision and Prayer" dwells on and in a moment, like this. Each is a lucid and usually simple poem whose steplike pattern, moving us up and down the diamond, in section I, or the hourglass, stylized as two triangles in a reordered diamond, in section II, rapidly tells its short story, and also visually seems to speed up the reading, like fast-motion shots in Thomas's beloved art of film.

There is a sense of fluidity, visual and aural, even though the concreteness of such shape-poems may also seem to halt the reading, in an invitation to make a spatial survey. But the auditory imagination—or the actual ear, if the poem is read aloud—is invited to make a rapid movement. The stepping up and down of line lengths acts like a moving staircase, tipping us carefully over each line to the next, or a domino effect, or a neat row-by-row unraveling of knitted fabric. These brief shape-poems come to have a predictable structure. They also have a crystalline clarity, and one aspect of the clarity is the narrative speed into momentariness. If Thomas radically slowed up narrative in those image-clotted poems such as "Light breaks where no sun shines," where micronarrative rules and compensates, he did the opposite in these mystical and meditative poems, achieving an expressive and new form for an experience, or an imagined experience of seeming timelessness. We seem to go both quickly and slowly as time is made strange in the imagining of a timeless moment. Music is always important in Thomas's poetry, and in these poems it is functionally and oddly inseparable from the visually assertive shape: sound and shape go together as the lines run up and down, and the insistent full rhymes, half-rhymes, and internal rhymes emphasize and accelerate.

More obviously, the extreme musicalization of language is there again in a melting and merging of words in "A Winter's Tale," where the racing words make a fluent medium for excitement. The music is like flying, or like tumescence. Indeed, the movement of Thomas's words and lines, like that of Joyce's prose, is often sexual, like prolonged crescendo and strong climax in music—in Purcell, say, or Beethoven. Here the erotic movement is right for the subject:

> The sky, the bird, the bride,
> The cloud, the need, the planted stars, the joy beyond
> The fields of seed and the time dying flesh astride,
> The heavens, the heaven, the grave, the burying font.
> In the far ago land the door of his death glided wide,

> And the bird descended.

In this example the words run into each other, and overlap in sound and sense, as frequently happens in Hopkins's fluent, expansive, and elastic lines, for example in "The Golden Echo and the Leaden Echo," which Thomas liked, and liked to read aloud, in "Spelt from Sibyl's Leaves," and "That Nature is a Heraclitean Fire and of the Comfort of the Resurrection," whose long-line rhythmical flowings resonate through Thomas's work, and to many of whose onomatopoeic and run-together words he sounds golden echoes, for instance, "spell," "leaves," "flash," "crash" and "patch." Thomas sometimes claimed to admire fluidity of language, sometimes not, but it is central in his poetry, a source of new music and energy.

As I've said, in "Reminiscences of Childhood" (reprinted in QEOM) Thomas borrowed the first word in *Finnegans Wake*, the compressed, onomatopoeic, and nonce word, "river-run," which he used as an adjective but decompressed and reconventionalized as two words, "river run." Joyce himself owes something to the racing lines, puns, reduplications, vowel and consonant echo and permutation, and portmanteau mergings of Hopkins—whom Joyce echoes and quotes in *Finnegans Wake.* Here are two demonstrative lines, the first from "Spelt from Sibyl's Leaves," the second from *Finnegans Wake:*

> Earnest, earthless, attuneable, vaulty, voluminous. . . . stu-
> pendous
> Evening strains to be time's vast, womb-of-all, home-of-all,
> hearse-of-all-night

and

> Can't hear with the waters of. The chittering waters of. Flit-
> tering bats, fieldmice bawk talk.

Both extracts are examples of musical flow, and words edging into each other, and Joyce's second sentence is also an example of his nominal, verbless sentences, an important item in his fluent style.

Thomas also emulated Carroll and Joyce in the fluency of portmanteau words, though he chose a different metaphor for them, once praising Joyce's "concertina" method of compression, in a review of Eric Ambler's *Epitaph for a Spy* (EPW). "Concertina" is a perfect image for the springy elasticity of language, in Hopkins, Joyce and Thomas, which can achieve effects of compression, voluminous expansion, and sudden shifts from one to the other. These kinds of fluidity and asserted music often result, in all three writers, in a sound that outruns sense, poetry charming at the expense of enlightenment, appealing to what Coleridge—aware that we often enjoy poetry the more for not wholly understanding it—called our sense of musical delight. This is said to be a feature of traditional Welsh poetry. It is also what we experience, after all, when we listen to songless music, responding sensuously and emotionally but unable to put the meanings of communication into words. I do not mean that the poetry is the same as music, or to suggest that poetic meaning is unimportant, only that poetry, like music, may dim or hold up or inhibit or subvert the comprehensibility of total narratives and arguments we usually expect of literature. Literature may aspire to the condition of music but words can't easily or often reach that condition. Thomas, like Hopkins and Joyce, goes further in musical aspiration than most writers.

Along with this musicalization and word merging, this rewriting and restructuring of the poetic line, there is often a breaking, fragmentation and dilapidation, which obscure coherence, unity and progression. In Thomas it is often the parts or the fragments that are prominent, and that the reader grasps first. By "first" I don't mean prior to the musical appeal, with which, though distinct from it, it collaborates, but prior to, or disconnected from, an understanding of the whole. Sometimes we begin by reading the packed image parts independently of an obscure whole, which we can't follow through or sum up; we cling to the parts, and assemble them in themselves, often out of sequence. That can be said—perhaps should be said?—the other way round: perhaps what makes the whole so often appear, or actually be, inaccessible, obscured, and fractured, is this discrete assertion of the parts. Such assertiveness and fragmentation, or assertive fragmentation, is what *The Waste Land, Finnegans Wake,* many of the cubist paintings of Picasso and the surrealism of Magritte and Max Ernst, Thomas's "Altarwise by owl-light" sonnet sequence, "A Winter's Tale," and "The Ballad of the Long-legged Bait" all have in common. It is one of the most radical features of Thomas's modernist form. It is also a feature of much later poetry, like the work of John Ashbery or John Ash, but neither of these fascinating poets makes the strong sensuous music which accompanies, stresses, and charmingly disguises the narrative and thematic absences or floutings in Thomas.

There are several ways in which a localized image or meaning makes itself structurally conspicuous, undermining or

replacing teleological progression and unity. Thomas's images—similes, metaphors, synecdoches and personifications
usually presenting a visual or a tactile appeal, usually making
some sense impact—are complex. They tend to join particularized sensuousness with idea or abstraction, making the familiar strange or the strange familiar, or both. When writing
to Treece and Hansford Johnson, Thomas often dwells on his
fondness for combining body images with abstract concepts:
the poetic parts or units themselves, sensuously imaged concepts and abstracted particulars, are always, or almost always,
reasoned and coherent.

Perhaps the rational element in the image explains the
poet's frequently versed irritation or amusement at being
called surrealist (for instance, in CL, p. 282, and "Poetic
Manifesto," EPW). In fact the disclaimers were disingenuous,
because—as I mentioned in chapter 1—Thomas published in
Roger Roughton's *Contemporary Poetry and Prose*,[5] a magazine
which had a strongly surrealist bias. He also attended a surrealist congress at which he participated by offering people
cups of string. But you can see the difference between the
famous surrealist images and his verbal units. The cup of
string and the lobster telephone are jokes and oxymorons,
impossible images. Thomas's are more like the separate images in Magritte, though, which make perfect sense in themselves but are crazy or impossible or inaccessible to rational
analysis, in context: the apple is strange because it fills a
room, the stone birds because they're flying in the air.
Thomas's reader takes in the image or word rather than the
narrative totality, but that image or word is lucid. Many surrealists, like André Breton, for instance, aimed at relaxing
consciousness and opening the way for the irrational, and the
uncontrolled, whereas Thomas, as Treece valuably insisted,
though like the surrealists in letting a flow of images "make
themselves" for him, was most unlike them in his declared
attempt to apply "to his images what intellectual and critical

forces he possesses, allowing them to exist only within certain formal limits" (TR, p. 27).

One form of dislocation which makes some poems look more surreal than they are is a disruption of the logical or chronological order of image elucidation. In "I make this in a warring absence," for instance, there is a highly obscure metaphor-packed first stanza:

I make this in a warring absence when
Each ancient, stone-necked minute of love's season
Harbours my anchored tongue, slips the quaystone,
When, praise is blessed, her pride in mast and fountain
Sailed and set dazzling by the handshaped ocean,
In that proud sailing tree with branches driven
Through the last vault and vegetable groyne,
And this weak house to marrow-columned heaven,

Is corner-cast, breath's rag.

This is one of the few poems Thomas explained, though only in a general way, saying—I paraphrase his paraphrase—that it was about hostile absence and transient truce-making presence, a destruction of sexual pride in union, and the self-destructive regression of a warring beloved, with the expectation of repeated war and peace (CP, p. 216). We may or may not well get this gist as we read: the problem with some poems we call obscure is the detail, the individual steps in a reading, the relation of part to whole. In Thomas these are not usually obscure, but offer separate, sometimes provisional, or unresolved, meanings.

One source of obscurity in the word-by-word, image-by-image scanning process is Thomas's compression and compounding of different and unexpected kinds of disorder. Here, for instance, is the juxtaposition of two syntactical forms in deceptive relationship: in "Harbours my anchored tongue, slips the quaystone," the first verb, "harbours," is attached by an absent but understood relative "which" to "season" and tells us about past harboring, while the second, "slips," is not, as it seems, in apposition to "harbours" but governed by the subject "minute" and tells us about the departure: apparently parallel forms diverge. And this obscuring construction is compounded by another of Thomas's favorite postponements of meaning, within the clause or within the sentence. In this case the sentence is two eight-line stanzas long, and the poem makes us wait, retarding elucidation while offering packed images which have, or seem to have, temporarily satisfactory but ultimately misleading meanings. The meaning, for instance, of a love called "stone-necked," is at first obscure, and probably misread as "stubborn," but after we read the next few lines, and modify "stone-necked" with the subsequent images of "harboured" and "anchor," we come up with the final meaning of strength and security. In the first stanza we receive images of exultation, "praise be blessed," and "Sailed and set dazzling," then, in the second stanza, and not till then, we begin to guess at a meaning of loss, in "corner-cast" with its riddling suggestions of a cast cornerstone, to find this confirmed in the clearer though new and clashingly compounded image "breath's rag." These examples show how the poem—like many of his poems—must be rescanned, reread, and reanalyzed, and the usual sequential process of elucidation inhibited or put into reverse.

The stories within the story sometimes make the poem as a whole a kind of anthology or cluster. Instead of the narrative as a whole giving the reader something to distract attention, as Thomas suggested, while the "essence"—let us substitute emotion?—works on us, the narratives on the way, within the images, do something of the kind, at best complicating and elaborating, providing jokes and puzzles. This is certainly the way most readers still read the obscure, and much explicated, ten-sonnet sequence, "Altarwise by owl-light." Some of its riddling images require less than half a minute's thought, like the "two bark towers" of Sonnet X, others a little longer, especially for readers used to unraveling the layers of allusion in Eliot and Joyce:

> With priest and pharaoh bed my gentle wound,
> World in the sand, on the triangle landscape,
> With stones of odyssey for ash and garland
> And rivers of the dead around my neck.
> (IX)

In "stones of odyssey" and "rivers of the dead around my neck" we find examples of deceptive allusion, in which we may get trapped or unnecessarily involved. The first may be read as the Phaeacian ship turned to stone by Poseidon after Odysseus finally lands in Ithaca, the second to the river Styx's behavior when Pluto tried to cross with the live and abducted Persephone. But both actually make better sense if we ignore the deeper allusions and stay with their superficial image-meanings, as Thomas sometimes seems to say his readers should. So stones are images of the hard journey, exhaustion and labor replacing funeral rite and laureate praise, "ash and garland" (a hendiadys joining live tree and leafy tribute, nature and art); the rivers of the dead around the neck, mere millstone-weighing deadly ancestries. (In this respect Thomas is not like Joyce, whose classical allusions can scarcely be too deeply plumbed. Thomas was well read in the Bible and English literature, less well acquainted with Homer.)

Thomas often jammed together images unrelated in origin, theme, and register. But the image may constitute the whole poem, not just forming or occupying a part or producing a local effect. One of Thomas's most obscure poems is the much-discussed "Where once the waters of your face," a poem which always comes to mind when I stand now in the famous Cwmdonkin Park where the famous waters of the railed-in reservoir—bombed out of existence in World War II—once shone between the bushes. It is as if the poem were prophetic, foreseeing an aridity which postdated the writing: if it had not, it's easy to see how critics would have explained the poem, in spite of the salt associations. My brother, Bill Nathan, tells me the reservoir often seemed "to seethe and boil," like water churned by a boat's propeller (screw), and this may even have suggested the image:

> Where once the waters of your face
> Spun to my screws, your dry ghost blows,
> The dead turns up its eye;
> Where once the mermen through your ice
> Pushed up their hair, the dry wind steers
> Through salt and root and roe.

But it was not prophetic, not about drying of the fresh and then un–dried up park waters. It is a poem which creates an indecision about the relationship of vehicle (the image carrier) and the tenor (the meaning carried). Is it a love poem in which the loss of human or nonhuman or superhuman love is metaphorically illustrated by the dried-up waters, or the reverse, a nature poem in which a dried-up riverbed or stream is represented by amorous and religious symbols? The poem raises the question but doesn't answer it. What we read is the image, its alternative meanings oscillating, suspended, and open. We have to accept a vehicle (or background) constantly changing places with tenor (or foreground). Meaning is not stably determined, but the imagery is characteristically sensuous and abstract, grotesque and rational.

Within this ambiguous and shifting story, some of the details are locally clear, and independent, behaving like my paradigmatic surrealist examples from Magritte. The image of "The green unraveller" in the second stanza is an image of destruction, but we have already been told that destruction has taken place, because the poem puts everything in the past. The unraveller doesn't clear up meanings, because he is said to be active in the present, so there is a logical contradiction of that pastness. He is a variant of one of Thomas's favorite characters, the scissorman from *Struwwelpeter*, here easily identified, grotesque, traditional, sensuous and precise. Character image is complete in itself, set in motion with "there goes," and given solidly imagined working accouterments, "His scissors oiled, his knife hung loose." The locally vivid character denotes a necessary and customary destruction, but it doesn't have much to do emotionally with either interpretation, rather moving away from the emotional emphasis which is so strong, the sense of loss and survival, plain and strong whether it is a loss of human love or of something treasured in nonhuman nature. The unraveller starts off a little story of his own, belonging to its own narrative register: a creature made strangely but naturally green, an underwater marine engineer with his tools and also a green man, green knight, or *wodwo*, bent on his death-life vegetation rites. (Thomas may or may not have known that shape-changing Gawain has features of a vegetation myth). The detail is a micronarrative, invoking literary and mythological associations, but reconstructing a figure with new meaning and emotional impact, sinister and benign. We seem to move into this image as into a cul-de-sac: it can be forced into a New Critical interpretation of a whole—whichever interpretation we choose—but it is really arresting in its own right, and it offers a pocket of intelligibility within the larger obscurity of the whole poem.

This is also an eddying poem, with the third stanza not advancing the story or feeling but accruing fresh images of what is said at the beginning. The end is strong, in its anticipation and assertion, but we remain, I think, with the oscillation of meanings: is this loss of human love or loss of a treasured time or loss of a beloved spot in nature?

There shall be corals in your beds,
There shall be serpents in your tides,
Till all our sea-faiths die.

Perhaps it begins to seem like a poem about the need and strength of imagination, another reflexive story and set of images. If so, it depends on the instability: we don't know what has been lost, only that it has been valued and can be revered, in a way, by imagination. The particulars remain disturbingly abstract, the abstractions oddly particular.

A similar abstraction and particularity and a separate local assertion are strikingly interinanimated in the following images from different difficult poems: "the brawned womb's weathers" (in "I see the boys of summer in their ruin"); "the shabby curtains of the skin" (in "A process in the weather of the heart"); "And mother milk was stiff as sand" (in "Where once the twilight locks no longer"); a comparison of the heart to "a naked Venus" treading "The beach of flesh" and winding her "bloodred plait" (in "My hero bares his nerves"); and the more obvious, but brilliant, "a candle in the thighs" (in "Light breaks where no sun shines"). All the figures work through likeness and unlikeness. The same could be said of most similes (Burns's "My love is like a red red rose," for instance) and metaphors (Hopkins's "the mind . . . has mountains") but my chosen set from Thomas uses the common mixture with more than usual unlikeness. In them all, extremes meet.

The womb is visualized naturalistically and precisely as a mottled marbled lump of brawn (a favorite Welsh working-class food, often on display in the windows of what used to be called "Welsh-shops," selling Welsh produce, usually cooked meats), but the gap between vehicle and tenor is a gap between life's matrix and dead meat. The transformation of milk to sand works rather differently, impossibility being logical, imaged as a nourishing mammal's liquid is turned into a gritty unnourishing mineral, the stuff of deserts, in a perfected opposition. The heart is oddly but aptly imaged as Venus, in a revision of Botticelli's braided Aphrodite (a favorite of Thomas's, hung or nailed, like Chagall, on his wall) a strange bringing together of a whole with a part, goddess with organ, but an organ mythologized, like the person, Venus, as symbol of the affections, and the color bloodred working perfectly in its two ways.

The odd one out in this series is "the shabby curtains of the skin," which works less through dissimilarity than likeness, but the narrative process or image story is there, slowly grasped as we proceed through that first shock at the oddity of the comparison to a wry recognition of the appositeness of both parts of the image: our flimsy flesh does indeed wear out quickly, and become very shabby, old, dirty, creased, and flabby, and is too easily drawn back, in illness or decay. The skin's shabbiness is a distressing image of mortality.

Such tropes work through making a bizarre approach to oxymoron, accompanied by a rational retreat from it. Brawn is made of flesh and nourishes. Mother milk is its opposite (solid) when it is uncreated, as it is in the poem's tale and time. In each image vehicle and tenor are both physical, both precise. Opposites are married by wit or conceit to engender new emblematic hybrid creatures, brawn-womb, sand-milk, heart-Venus, like Magritte's stone-birds or face-torso. There is a marked resemblance in these examples to surrealist imagery, but Thomas's images are more intelligible and rational, improbable rather than impossible. Their initial impact may seem irrational, but they succumb to intelligent questioning.

That questioning takes time, and involves going out on a narrative limb, patiently and piecemeal reading the story of the image, which is often discrete, isolated, digressive, and always time-consuming. Unlike the story of the poem as a whole, which may resist the rational probes, it gives an answer—tentative, segregated, shifting—to some questions.

3. Dramatic, Narrative, Lyric

Across the Genres

In the twelfth poem of *18 Poems*, 1934, "From Love's First Fever," Dylan Thomas speaks of learning

> man's tongue, to twist the shapes of thoughts
> Into the stony idiom of the brain,
> To shade and knit anew the patch of words
> Left by the dead.

Thomas was a language changer, and fully aware of it, one of those rare artists who resourcefully quarry the riches of the language to make it his own. In his case what he took was a miscellany, though confined to the English language, literary and demotic, mined from poetry, novel, film, drama, sermons, psalms, hymns, urban and rural dialects, slang, traditional periphrasis, and swearword, molded into something new and individual, capable of articulating and forming his mind, passions, sensations, fantasy and experience. His form and language resemble those of other writers, most conspicuously his immediate predecessors and contemporaries, Gerard Manley Hopkins, T. S. Eliot, and above all James Joyce, an important model for language, narrative form, and ironic national feeling. Thomas is modern, indeed modernist, but at his best, he re-creates forms and languages in ways expressive of his deep self, most visibly of his time, but becoming one of the great individualists of modern art.

When Coleridge read Wordsworth's "Boy of Winander-Mere" in 1798 he said of one of its lines that if he met it running wild in the desert it would scream out "Wordsworth." Coleridge's metaphor for recognizing unmistakable individuality fits Thomas even better than Wordsworth, not because Thomas is a more individually expressive poet—he's not—but because he is more idiosyncratic, working more on the fringe of language. And also because that wild image of the word running wild and screaming suits his wildness so well. He was of course wild in some ways that Wordsworth—whom Thomas underrated—might have found distasteful. When in the villanelle written to his father, "Do not go gentle into that good night," Thomas speaks of the wild men who "caught and sang the sun in flight, / And learn, too late, they grieved it on its way," he is speaking as a man acquainted with wildness. But what is important is that, like Wordsworth, his voice is a signature, a voice that you recognize when you hear it, a voice that couldn't belong to anyone else.

He changes language for himself, and he changes it across several genres: his first and last best genre, lyric poetry, in which he began to excel as a very young poet of fifteen, the short story, and the newer genres of radio play, screenplay, and broadcast radio. Because he finds a voice for his individuality, it can be the voice of whatever he says, including unscripted talks and letters, but he was capable of neutralizing and subduing that voice, complying with special needs and special occasions. But it can and does sound in all his genres. It is not a voice which sounds quite different in poetry—where it is most uninhibited and strong—and in prose. It is recognizably his voice except on the few odd occasions—in some of the film scripts, for instance—where he disguises it as everyone's or anyone's voice. Those are truly exceptions which prove a rule.

Dylan Thomas was a language changer like certain other strong individualists before him, and he is conspicuously drawn to some of these—Shakespeare, Dickens, Hopkins and Joyce. On one occasion Thomas denied Hopkins's influence but in an early essay ("Poetic Manifesto," first published in *Texas Quarterly*, vol. 4, no. 4, and reprinted in EPW) he said Hopkins was the greatest single influence on modern English literature. These are all writers, of different periods and writing in different genres, whose individual language changes and language strangeness he loved, assimilated, and made his own. Like theirs, his style is self-expressive but also self-conscious, in a way that intensifies and does not inhibit.

Shakespeare, Dickens, Hopkins, Joyce and Thomas all write in ways which show, implicitly and explicitly, that they know what they are doing. One of the pleasures of studying Thomas's original language in poetry, story, and drama is to respond to passion, sensuousness, and intelligent self-awareness. That conspicuous, often central, act of self-awareness is one of his claims to modernism, making him one of the innovators in self-consciousness, with such artists as Joyce, Lawrence, Woolf, Picasso and Messiaen. Like these, he was a breaker and unmaker, as well as maker, of forms and styles.

But he is also a language changer for all of us, readers and writers. His language has imperceptibly changed whatever is meant by the written English language, certainly in Wales, where it has become difficult to write poetry without traces or echoes of Thomas. It can change language because it is itself new, recognizable and original, and after it has been heard and read the English language is never quite the same again. Joyce said that Dickens entered into the language.[1] This judgment becomes applicable to Joyce himself, and then again to Dylan Thomas. The language of poetry, and perhaps of prose too, has been enriched by his originality, and also by his intelligence, because he is aware, and because he makes us aware, of language's growth and capacity. Thomas shows its action and energy by his practice and his analysis. He is a great lyric poet but he articulated the self in several media, which fed into each other, and did not stay self-contained and separate. Like Joyce and Katherine Mansfield, but almost no other contemporary writer of stories, he brought lyricism into short fiction, where his success is remarkable. Some of his screenplays are excellent, but the most famous and accessible of his writings belongs to the popular medium so important in the thirties and forties when he was growing up in Wales and becoming a poet—the radio.

His last work, finished and performed just before, and published after, his early death in 1953, is *Under Milk Wood*, the play for voices whose title is so original and strange that it is still found teasing, and which has had wide sales, readings and performances. As his first narrator says more than once, "Listen," in this case to the Second Voice:

> Gossamer Beynon high-heels out of school. The sun hums down through the cotton flowers of her dress into the bell of her heart and buzzes in the honey there and couches and kisses, lazy-loving and boozed, in her red-berried breast. (p. 60)

and

> she whispers to her salad-day deep self. (p. 60)

and

> she tells the stripped and mother-of-the-world big-beamed and Eve-hipped spring of her self. (p. 60)

It is a story, a drama, and poetic prose. It is written to be listened to, and strongly marked in rhythm and visual imagery. It is also dense with literary allusion, and this extract clearly remembers Shakespeare and Joyce, both of whom Thomas praised. In his "Poetic Manifesto" (EPW) he said he "enormously admired" Joyce, whose stories Thomas more or less admitted were a model for his, and whose fluid prose is a major influence on his poetry. In the piece "Idioms" he compared his own "bellow of X, Y, and Z, with a few childish frills," with Shakespeare's "roaring majesty" (EPW). Here Thomas shows how he has become saturated in that language, daring to use it again, conspicuously using Shakespeare's most sexual woman's brilliant metaphor, "salad days," which was also a neologism and a compounding, and in a way which fits in perfectly with the daring metaphors, neologisms and compoundings Thomas makes up for himself, "lazy-loving," "red-berried," "Eve-hipped," all confident in their company. No anxiety of influence here but fun, pride, and admiration, the celebration of a common craft and wit.

But there is more to this salad-day deep self than playful homage. High-heeling Gossamer is one of several spirited heroines, each with her own language—Polly Garter, Mrs. Ogmore-Pritchard, the two Mrs. Dai Breads, Mary Ann Sailors, and Rosy Probert—in this highly sexual comedy. Thomas is no feminist, and his celebrations of woman, like Joyce's, are in some ways conventional and sentimental, but the woman's vitality and cheek can almost—I stress, almost—make us forget this. Gossamer's style remembers her ancestresses, salad-day remembering queen and goddess Cleopatra and rose-remembering earth-mother Molly Bloom, each more powerful than ordinary women but in touch with ordinariness. The erotic language is inventive and daring, and the novelties of language are as typical of Thomas as they were of Shakespeare and Joyce. Close to them too is the free-flowing prose, carrying on the inventive words, compounds, and images in a trajectory, or what Thomas calls a "progress" of sensation and feeling. It is a bouncy, buoyant, bawdy language, a sensuous and appreciative style for the sensuous and appetitive character. Exuberance and joy are subject and style.

But Gossamer is airier than the Egyptian queen who declares that she is fire and air, because another more ethereal Shakespearean character went into her making, the wild and lissome high-flying Ariel who sucked with the bee in a cowslip bell just as Thomas's sun sucks in the honey of Gossamer's heart. Thomas is a great poet of the sun, like Chagall, one of his favorite painters, whose tender sensibility, grotesque fantasy, flower-and-beast mergers, and rainbow palette Thomas often recalls. In this passage the sun is species-crossed with the bee to make a sharp erotic image. (It is also entirely in keeping with Thomas's insistence on the unity of being, though in the context of this lighthearted play such a reference sounds inept and heavy.)

Gossamer's name, like her nature, and like so many and so much in the play, is divided, one half ordinary and demotic, the other poetic and ethereal. "Gossamer" is air and flower, "Beynon" a good common South Welsh surname. This is where her ancestress Molly Bloom comes in, another Celtic creation, another man-made sex object with a difference, another woman with a double name and nature, "Molly," a solid, menstruating, chamber-pot-using, copulating Irishwoman, and "Bloom," a flower of the mountain, all roses on Howth Hill in the summer. Gossamer Beynon is right for the lightness and prettiness of the neat little schoolmistress, ordinary and familiar as she high-heels out of school. Even the sun in *Milk Wood* is ordinary and familiar as it boozes in those most sensual but transformed breasts, which are milky animal and strange as they nourish the sun, new and vegetable with their red berry nipples. And once more, a swirl and mingling of human, nonhuman, vegetable and mineral. Mother of the world and containing all the springs—the season, the spring in her step, the source of water, and the coiled energy of the deep self, Gossamer is Eve and Cleopatra and Molly Bloom, but Dylan Thomas's version, double personality, prim teacher and sexy fantasist. Hers is one amongst many lyrical voices in the chorus telling—like Joyce—a story of one day and something of the night in a small community. The radio play for many voices, joining and separating, dramatizing and narrating is, as Walford Davies shows in his introduction to the recent (1995) Dent and Everyman editions, Thomas's lighthearted but triumphant Welsh *Ulysses.* And we can apply to the gentle eroticism of *Under Milk Wood* what the judge John M. Woolsey famously said of Joyce's *Ulysses* when he decided it should not be banned in the United States: we should remember that the season is spring and the locale Celtic.

The exuberance of the play for voices should not blind us to its subtlety. The debt to Joyce—not only to *Ulysses* but also to the great and poetic novel of the night, *Finnegans Wake*—is a complex and brilliant achievement, very like Joyce's debt to Homer, only much more laid back and unobtrusive. (It has been discussed but not fully perceived, in his drama, lyric, or fiction.)

In *Under Milk Wood* Joyce is there in the characters, he's there in the time scheme, he's there in the dream fantasy, he's there in the narrative monologues, he's there in the fun and flow. And just as Joyce's great Homeric celebration changes the way we read *The Odyssey*, so perhaps Dylan Thomas's sprightly and comic play can lighten the way we read Joyce, whose comedy is sometimes neglected. Thomas's last work is much more ambitious than he ever let on—perhaps more than he ever knew. Whether its allusiveness is always conscious or not, it is present everywhere.

Under Milk Wood is a play in which narrative dominates, and in a way very unusual in drama at the time, and the modernist reliance on narrators is characteristic of the poet whose own voice was such a powerful and sensitive instrument. In the first reading/performance in New York, 1953, he read the parts of one narrator, and the ironic sympathy and exotic stylistic indulgence of the narration brings it close to the voice of his successful broadcasts, many of which, like "Reminiscences of Childhood" (TB) are gems of oral art, and examples of a mastery of the new medium. (In their recent edition of the play, Walford Davies and Ralph Maud adopt and defend Thomas's early conception of a single "First Voice" narrator, and their single strand of narration is typographically set off and distinguished from the dialogue by the italics of stage direction. In my quotations I have preferred Daniel Jones's earlier revised edition of 1974—despite faults which Davies and Maud reveal—in which two narrators appear, typographically, structurally, and theatrically merged with and undifferentiated from the other characters and voices in the stories they tell and introduce.)

Like *Under Milk Wood*, the broadcast scripts at their best show the common flowing lyric form, generating energy and emotion. The narrative thread, on which small events and descriptions are loosely slung, proceeds with the florid inventive recompounding of word, phrase, and image, the same patterns of assonance, alliteration, and rhyme that we find in the play, and of course even more intensively in the poetry. Thomas revised his talk "Reminiscences of Childhood" two years after it was broadcast in 1943, and here is the beginning of the unrevised and more "impulsive" version (as Ralph Maud, who edited and collected the talks, rightly describes it):

> I was born in a large Welsh industrial town at the beginning of the Great War: an ugly, lovely town (or so it was, and is, to me), crawling, slummed, unplanned, jerry-villa'd, and smug-suburbed by the side of a long and splendid-curving shore where truant boys and sandfield boys and old anonymous men, in the tatters and hangovers of a hundred charity suits, beachcombed, idled, and paddled, watched the dock-bound boats, threw stones into the sea for the barking, outcast dogs, and, on Saturday summer afternoons, listened to the militant music of salvation and hell-fire preached from a soap-box. This sea-town was my world; outside, a *strange* Wales, coal-pitted, mountained, river-run. (TB, p. 3)

I have mentioned the rhetorical similarity of Thomas's broadcast talks and the language of *Milk Wood*, but this radio talk is obviously a much quieter and more subdued prose passage than the Second Voice's account of Gossamer B (her lover's version of her comic-poetic name). The neat compoundings, though not startling or even conspicuous, are still novel and clever, keeping close to the model or analogue, in "jerry-villa'd" (for jerry-built), "coal-pitted," "slummed," "smug-suburbed" and "mountained" (participle back-formations from the noun form), and the Joycean "river-run" (from *Finnegans Wake*, more than once repeated by Thomas). The music isn't fully apparent until the words are read aloud, when their rhythms and rhymes come fully alive: "crawling, sprawling" and "idled and paddled." The idly beginning, ruminative stream of consciousness quietly serves the purpose of a colloquial and spontaneous-seeming act of memory: this is the beginning of a drama of the mind moving from voluntary generalizing reminiscence to involuntary recall, and as we proceed the descriptions and anecdotes move faster, the emotions get stronger, the imagery more intense, and at the end, wilder and more fantastic. Indeed, Thomas hardly ever wrote anything which wasn't in some way extravagant and hyperbolic—as for Dickens, exaggeration is Thomas's idiolect and medium—but in these talks he apparently takes care to begin on level ground, then gradually rise. And as every actor and public speaker knows, a loud sound comes better after quiet, a passionate emphasis after calm. Near the end the narrative swerves from past to present, merging memory and dream, yet still reminiscent, still recording the town, faithful to the excited free simple style of childhood:

Occasionally, now, I dream that I am turning, after school, into the lane of confidences where I say to the children of my class: "At last I have a secret."

"What is it? What is it?"

"I can fly!"

And when they do not believe me, I flap my arms like a large, stout bird and slowly leave the ground, only a few inches at first, then gaining ground till I fly, like Dracula in a schoolboy cap, level with the windows of the school, peering in until the mistress at the piano screams, and the metronome falls with a clout to the ground, stops, and there is no more Time, and I fly over the trees and the chimneys of my town, over the dockyards, skimming the masts and funnels; over Inkerman Street and Sebastopol Street and the street of the man-capped women . . . over the trees of the eternal Park. (TB, p. 7)

I was not surprised, and in some ways was relieved, to find that the very last sentence of the talk, "The fine, live people, the spirit of Wales itself" (TB, p. 8), was—according to Vernon Watkins—probably a politically pious conclusion "diplomatically added," though Watkins's information has been disputed (TB, pp. 1–2).

Thomas wrote for his own voice, but for others too, and not only in *Under Milk Wood* and the radio talks. Amongst the recent full collection of film scripts (as full as it can be at the moment, though more screenplays may turn up) is what is his most ambitious and successful screenplay. "Our Country," a long commentary in free verse, for narrators and characters, and one of many pieces which seems to be rehearsing the classic play for voices in *Milk Wood*. The correspondence about this film shows Thomas's scrupulous attention to craft and structure: for example, he carefully arranged that in the premiere the commentary should not be presented to the audience in a full written program, which might not only anticipate the visual images, but would be separated from them, to "suggest an artiness that is not in the film," and appear too modern (FS, p. 65). Like the "Reminiscences of Childhood," it is quiet writing, wit and lyricism subdued to the cinematic medium where the visualization is not the responsibility of the writer, as of course it is in all the other media in which

Thomas was working. He sometimes wrote disparagingly about his work for cinema, but practiced his new craft with pleasure, and did not regard it as hack work.

For instance, he took great care to create the verse continuity, faithfully constructed as contribution and collaboration, subordinated to the dominantly scenic art, and of course sometimes sacrificed to editorial cuts. In the following passage the sense of continuity is clear. The scriptwriter is providing an accompaniment to what the introductory program described as "real" scenes, shots of blitzed streets and buildings, and the extract immediately follows a shot of St. Paul's Cathedral, from which it takes the striking metaphor of a cathedral, used to signify a human body:

> And all the stones remember and sing
> the cathedral of each blitzed dead body that lay or lies
> in the bomber-and-dove-flown-over cemeteries
> of the dumb heroic streets.
>
> ("Our Country," screenplay written for a Ministry of Information film of that name, 1945, FS, p. 68)

Occasions of public grief are hard to lament without emotional excess or cold formality. This was the time of the numerous German air raids on British cities, in which there were many civilian casualties, as well as the loss of fine historic buildings like Coventry Cathedral. Thomas somehow manages to subdue but still use and modulate his individual voice in the generalized language of social grief. Behind the piece was his experience of the Swansea blitz, which he saw from just outside the town, in Bishopston, close but rural and unscathed, and which he lamented, "Our Swansea is dead," and his work fire watching in the London raids.

In his wartime screenplays, usually in prose, Thomas was writing propaganda for the British Ministry of Information, functionally simple in its designed appeal, and sometimes, for instance in a film designated to recruit women for barrage balloon sites, using a prose carefully neutralized and drained of individuality. But "Our Country," though scarcely plumbing the depths of patriotism, enthusiasm, and faith in the war, none of which Thomas felt, is a good example of his adaptation of skill and wit and poetry for a commissioned piece of propaganda. The poetic screenplay was produced for foreign consumption, and its "Introduction" was written by Sam Spewack to be spoken by an American serviceman based in the U.K. He presented "a picture about Britain. . . . the people are real. . . . the scenes are real" (FS, p. 64). It is not insincere, because articulating pity and respect for the dead had no political significance for the always death-obsessed Thomas, who satirically—though also with grim and ironic intent—described his narrator in the story "One Warm Saturday" as "a young man in touch with his maggots."

The literal, metaphorical and synecdochic images, like "cemetery of the streets," and "dumb heroic streets," are common in his poetry too but here they have a special effect because of the double application to those "real" scenes. The streets really became cemeteries (stone burial places), were of course dumb, and became heroic, so the rhetoric is subdued and earthed to ordinary actuality, plain and straight, neither litotes nor hyperbole. The vivid common naturalized war slang, nonchalantly borrowed from the enemy language, "blitzed" from "blitzkrieg," is a word Thomas uses several times, and here it is yoked with that of the dignifying metaphor of "cathedral," literalized by the proximity of actual bombed cathedrals. Cathedrals were casualties as well as people but Thomas is using a traditional image of a house or building as metaphor for the body, as in Shakespeare and Herbert.

The characteristic compound "dove-and-bomber-flown-over" is like Shakespeare and Hopkins as it links peace and war, and also echoes the key image of T. S. Eliot's *Little Gidding*, published three years before, in 1942. In his introduction to the screenplays John Ackerman rightly draws attention to Thomas as "our first, and first great civilian war-poet" (FS, x.). "Our" first is accurate—and so is "great"—but perhaps priority should be given to Eliot, whose air-raid symbols are clearly recalled here, and who was like Thomas well acquainted with London's air raids as a resident and as a fire watcher.

Thomas is inventively bringing together contraries, but also truthfully responding to the facts of war, subduing his voice, but writing vividly, and drawing easily on the literary traditions. The impressiveness of these scripts is their individuality, muted but active, and as so often, aware or making us aware of the literary roots of his plain—though not all that plain—style.

His most successful and original achievement, next to that of the poetry, is as a short-story writer. Though he wrote stories before and after *Portrait of the Artist as a Young Dog*, it is his outstanding work in prose fiction, both as a unified structure and as a collection of his best stories. Once more, the highly individual talent is visibly and admittedly nourished by its literary traditions. *Portrait of the Artist as a Young Dog* has a form and affective pattern which derived from Joyce. Thomas said the title was encouraged by the publishers as a moneymaking device, but in the event it was partly an acknowledgment, and partly a disguise, of the real source and model. The title makes it look as if it were modeled on Joyce's *Portrait of the Artist as a Young Man,* and it has a complex and muted developmental structure which to some extent seems to follow that model, but actually, as Thomas admitted, the important influence was Joyce's earlier work, the volume of short stories about his birthplace, *Dubliners:*

Dubliners was a pioneering work in the world of the short story and no good storywriter since, can have failed, in some way, however little, to have benefited from it. ("Poetic Manifesto," EPW)

How did Dylan Thomas's storytelling benefit? Joyce's self-contained stories about Dublin have some unity and continuity, but are held together by theme and place rather than characters. There is some trace of a developmental structure, since the early stories are about childhood, adolescence, and personal life, while the later ones are about maturity and public life. The early stories like "Araby," "The Sisters," and "An Encounter" have a young boy at the center, and concern themselves with creativity and fantasy as the later ones do not, extricating themselves from autobiographical themes in order to concentrate on scrupulously dramatizing the mean lives of the Dubliners, described by Joyce as morally paralyzed but managing to assert some individuality and innerness. The last story, "The Dead," returns us to a Joycean central figure and the subject of imagination. The developmental pattern and themes of Thomas's book are strikingly similar but certainly not identical.

The Welsh stories begin in childhood and progress to young manhood, keeping much closer to an autobiographical and personal progress or process. As in Joyce's *Portrait of the Artist as a Young Man,* but not in his collection of stories, there is a central concern with creativity, and a strong continuous line of artistic development, though this is subdued, not evolutionary, and the book ends with ambition, promise, and essay, not certain achievement. There is one narrator character, sometimes called "Dylan" and "Mr. Thomas" and sometimes nameless, who appears in all the stories, usually as spectator, witness, and recorder, but in three stories as a writer—the autobiographical "The Fight" and "Where Tawe Flows," and the fantastic concluding story, "One Warm Saturday." In "The Fight," "Who Do You Wish Was With Us?" (and a later story, "The Followers," not in the collection), the narrator is paired with a friend, another young dog from Swansea.

Like Joyce, Thomas uses a unity of place, making the region not only a common location but also thematic, a place to be described and defined, developed, felt for, and to some extent summed up, or even judged, as a social organism and a historic scene. He uses Swansea, its rural peninsula of Gower, and Fernhill farm in Carmarthenshire.

As in Joyce, the emphasis is also on mean lives, as far as poverty and ennui and misery go, but there is much more inner richness in many of the characters, and the social organism as a whole is certainly not suffering from moral paralysis, though the theme of a depressed and depressing community isn't entirely irrelevant to such stories as "One Warm Saturday" and even "The Peaches." *Under Milk Wood* is Thomas's *Ulysses* and his rite of spring, but his Swansea, unlike Joyce's Dublin, though once described by Thomas as a little Dublin, is not a mean place dramatized and described with scrupulous meanness. On the contrary. Joyce dramatizes a low-flickering creativity even in his drab Dubliners but though Thomas shows ordinary people, he likes to show them as extraordinary. Moreover, his volume of stories, unlike Joyce's, was written after Joyce's great exuberant novels had overtaken their author's experience and theme of provincial meanness. Joyce said he found Dublin a center of moral paralysis but Thomas said Swansea was the most romantic town he knew. And Thomas did not share Joyce's hostility to religion, nor his deep detestation of conventional family life. He had his nets to fly, but fewer of them, and he flew back more regularly, on many creative return journeys.

Like Joyce in the novels, though not in the stories, Thomas allows other characters to be as imaginative as himself, or as his narrator self. There are wretched characters like Ann and her drunkard husband in "The Peaches," the depressed silly husbands in "Just Like Little Dogs," and the pathetic Old Garbo, all almost too downtrodden for creativity, though the young husbands muster enough energy to tell their odd tawdry tale of hit-and-miss coupling and marrying. But there are other minor characters who are more imaginative and articulate storytellers. There is the powerful Gwilym, Dylan's cousin in "The Peaches," the randy poet and effusive preacher who gives a touch of his quality in the scene where he delivers a powerful sermon, *hwyl* and all, from a farm cart. And there is the narrator's friend, Raymond Price (closely modeled on Thomas's friend Trevor Hughes, already mentioned as Thomas's confidant about his aunt's illness), whose imagination plays a very important part in "Who Do You Wish Was With Us?"

The crucial but typical stories of Gwilym and Raymond are two threads in a cumulative and usually implicit pattern of creativity. The theme of imagination is the strongest cohering force in the book, making its shape, its theme, and its unity. Using an understated plotting which is Joycean (also in some ways Chekovian), Thomas makes it his own by forming many of the plots—not all—as vehicles for an original construction of observation and creativity. One of the fascinating aspects of the book is the total assimilation of Joyce's powerful influence. Though Thomas was so young and in some ways intellectually inexperienced, he seems to have been so deeply, sensitively, and intelligently saturated in Joyce that his imitation—in the Renaissance sense of derivation from model or paradigm—became precociously intuitive, his literary readings and recognitions made profoundly personal and unconscious.

Thomas imagined imagination afresh. There is a rhythmically repeated shift, occurring in enough of the stories to make it a prominent structural feature, from a quotidian level of experience, which forms one plot, to an action of imaginative transformation, in another. The paradigm story, in other words, is the story within the story, and is the story of its narration and its narrator. There are links with other predecessors, as well as Joyce. "One Warm Saturday" and "Who Do You Wish Was With Us?" are like miniature versions of

The Great Gatsby, in which we have the story of Gatsby and the story of his observer and narrator, Nick Carraway, whose own story is both subdued to the telling and told by and in that telling. They are also like an earlier classic of the genre, Henry James's novel *Roderick Hudson,* in which Roderick's apparently central story turns out to be the story of its teller, Rowland Mallett. In both novels there is the fascination of characterized narration—we tell our own stories as we tell each other's the ambiguity of center—who is the hero?—and an elegant solution to problems of narrative point of view. It may seem a far cry from James and Fitzgerald to Thomas's everyday stories of Swansea life, but this is because he is such a neglected and underestimated writer of fictional prose. (When he described the contents of his father's library to Pamela Hansford Johnson, Henry James was one of the authors listed on Thomas's father's shelves.)

"Who Do You Wish Was With Us?" is the best example of this double and shifting point of view, one of the finest stories about creativity and imagination. And the original language is the medium in which the author, and his narrator, imagine imagination. The story on the surface is about a country outing, a walk and bus ride from Swansea across a stretch of wild common to Rhossilli, one of the most beautiful Gower bays, distinguished by five miles of golden sand and a huge tidal island, already mentioned, snaking into the channel like a sea serpent and appropriately named the Worm's Head.

The characters, a nameless narrator and his companion, Raymond Price, are based on Dylan Thomas and Trevor Hughes, a slightly older friend, also ambitious to be a writer, to whom Thomas wrote interesting letters of admiration, encouragement and advice. In the story Raymond, or Ray, is a clerk in the GWR (Great Western Railway) whose mother is crippled and chair-bound, and whose father, sister, and brother have all died of tuberculosis, a familiar social scourge, product of poverty and poor hygiene, in South Wales in the first half of the century, until the discovery of streptomycin just after the Second World War. (Ray mentions his sister's sanitarium, Craigynos, a well-known hospital for tuberculosis outside Swansea.) It is a story in which compassion and empathy are movingly dramatized: at one point the narrator says he has "more love" in him than he can "ever want or use," and this is a story of loving friendship which has a social and an aesthetic dimension.

It is a story for which we have interestingly revealed sources, stated and implied in one or two of the letters Thomas wrote after Hughes left Swansea. The correspondence overlaps with the letters to Pamela Hansford Johnson, and Hughes, whose writing Thomas liked and encouraged, was, like her and like Vernon Watkins, a valued friend and creative equal with whom he exchanged ideas and experiences. Thomas got to know Hughes, as a potential contributor, when he was planning to start a new literary magazine for Welsh writing in English. (*Wales* fulfilled Thomas's cultural dream, but though he coedited one early number with his friend Keidrych Rhys, and contributed poems, he tried to suppress his name from the title page.)

The letters written in 1932 and 1933 show several striking examples of what Coleridge famously called the "hooked atoms," bits of experience organized and fused into unity by imagination. In this case the hooked atoms are not images from literary sources, but from life: the actual miseries of the illness and bereavement which the older man had suffered, Thomas's strong sympathy, the creative inhibitions by grief and loss, and a recollection of the Rhossili landscape and its symbolism.

"What you want to keep out is morbidity, even though everything is despondent" (CL, p. 18); "Not that what you have suffered does not influence you deeply & terribly. It is bound to upset & disillusion, carry you, unless you are careful, to the margins of madness" (CL, p. 11); "Shun morbidity. . . . You say, or at least imply, that you couldn't because of your terrible misfortunes. And I say that you can. Morbidity is sickness, unhealthiness. That need to play no great part in your stories" (CL, p. 12); "I am interested in what you say about your story writing—the quick, quiet, dream-come idea, the lifting of the pen, & then the faces of past miseries and horrors obliterating everything. I can understand why your output is so small" (CL, p. 14); "Write a story . . . about yourself searching for your soul amid the horrors of corruption and disease" (CL, p. 16); "Come back to Wales" (CL, p. 18); and "Remember the Worm, read a meaning into its symbol—a serpent's head rising out of the clean sea" (CL, p. 18).

Thomas wrote the story, a story about them both. It was during this brief but intense and analytic correspondence that Thomas made his confession about feeling unmoved by his Aunt Ann's last illness. In his letters he is clearly writing both about his friend's creativity and his own—about creativity as a concept. Out of the introspection and the empathy comes the story. In it the symbol of the great serpentine headland is used, though with a difference. It dramatizes and uses the experiences of inhibiting morbidity and imaginative sympathy and the struggle for freedom and self-expression. The result of Thomas's generous encouraging attention to Hughes's story-writing was not a story by Hughes, but his own story about Hughes, and about their common experience of imagination. (Hughes was to provide another occasion and impetus for Thomas's art, in the poem "Foster the light," which I discuss in chapter 4.)

"Remember the Worm." The two young men, the schoolboy, based on Dylan but not called by any name in this story, and the older young clerk, based on Hughes, set off together for the Worm. They walk out from the town to the grass and gorse of the common which marks the end of Swansea and the beginning of Gower. After they succumb to the temptation of a passing bus, they get to Rhossilli, go on the long low-tide walk out to the tidal island of the Worm, and after spending some hours climbing its rocks and grassy plateau, are overtaken by the tide, and finally watch it cover the low rocks which join the headland to the Rhossilli mainland.

The day's journey forms the external action but it is the occasion, cause, and effect of a trajectory of feeling, composed of elation, sorrow, and pity, and produced by the transient release from the memory of suffering, the returning memory of suffering, and the compulsive story of Ray's beloved brother's suffering and death. The final arrival at the tide-covered causeway coincides with the story of the death, which the narrator is forced to hear. The incoming high water has isolated them and their telling and listening, and cut them off, to contemplate mortality.

It is also a story about place. The great ancient headland and island, at first nearly surrounded, and at the end totally surrounded, by sea and sky, is a place of freedom, but also a place of constraint, a place where contingency is briefly eluded, but finally and conclusively a place where time and place are found and felt to rule and restrain inexorably.

The feelings of holiday, physical energy, joy, and freedom, begin early, as the characters delight in their walk, in the escape from the town and its routines of time and work, and—honestly, unassumingly, but importantly—in wild nature. They aren't too knowledgeable about nature, and Thomas nicely cools pastoral ardors by making his narrator vague about the names of birds, and Ray only a little better informed. The pastoral ideal and refuge is realized, quietened, and made comic, by the tempting arrival of the bus and the hasty end of the long hike, in which they have taken some pride, looking down on the "townees." But they are just a couple of townees themselves. Thomas is controlling his romantic impulses and pastoral morality with wit and skill. His qualifications of pastoral are traditional rather than subversive: Shakespeare made Arden less than a glamorous ideal, as the refugees from court realize when their first shepherd explains that he tends another man's sheep and works hard.

The coolness and understatement of Thomas's story are preparing, and making a context, for powerful intensities. When the young men get to the Worm the sense of holiday and freedom returns, and is directly associated with the elements, rock and wind and sea. The experience is expressed with Thomas's imagistic power, but with a precision and lucidity not always found in his poetry. Poet, actor, and reader, he imagines for his narrator an exhilarating amplification of the voice, imaging the event synaesthetically, through a clever image of resonating space, one which keeps close to the register of confined and tangible sea things, "shell or cave," then imagines space as oxymoronically expansive, though using the actual sky's arch for a simile, then returns from fantasy to the real presence of the gulls, though amplifying their cry too, but in a realistic description of what gulls can sound like. He dares to use the common epithet "thunderous," which in the context is strange and also apt for the sea experience:

> On the point, the sound of my quiet voice was scooped and magnified into a hollow shout, as though the wind around me had made a shell or cave, with blue, intangible roof and sides, as tall and wide as all the arched sky, and the flapping gulls were made thunderous.

He is finding words for the extraordinary ecstatic experience we call—or used to call—the sublime, and he naturalizes it, in a way the great aestheticians of sublimity, Longinus and Kant, would have found congenial. He uses the large things in nature—sky, sea, and a massive isolatable rock headland—as Longinus recommends in *On the Sublime*, and his emotional seascape perfectly conforms to Kant's definition of the sublime as an experience which suspends our sense of comparison. It is also Longinian in its attempt to communicate a "lofty" concept and an intense feeling, as it goes on to image the experience of pushing at the boundary of the ego. It is true ecstasy, a going out of the self. It is what Arthur Koestler described as the oceanic feeling:

> Instead of becoming small on the big rock poised between sky and sea, I felt myself the size of a breathing building, and only Ray in the world could match my lovely bellow as I said: "Why don't we live here always? Always and always. Build a bloody house and live like bloody kings."

Dylan Thomas manages to express the ineffable feeling, or the feeling of ineffability, of the experience of ecstasy, in an unromantic and individualizing way which combines the language of the natural sublime with a plausible matter-of-factness, a controlled bathos, "the size of a . . . building," and colloquial crudeness, "bloody . . . bloody." The sublime is explained—but certainly not explained away—as a form of empathy, but those plans to build a house have an endearing touch of practical reality. (You understand why Thomas loved his writing shed and the Boathouse on the edge of the cliff at Laugharne: he was planning it on the Worm's Head.)

The passage goes on modulating:

> The word bellowed among the squawking birds, they carried it off to the headland in the drums of their wings; like a tower, Ray pranced on the unsteady edge of a separate rock and beat about with his stick, which could turn into snakes or flames; and then sank to the ground, the rubbery, gull-limed grass, the sheep-pilled stones, the pieces of bones and feathers, and couched at the extreme point of the Peninsula.

The prose jumps strenuously, with the energy and dynamism of the poetry, and stretches in sublime expansion, for instance, of "the word," in a way which very quietly makes it like a creative flat, like "the Word" in St. John, then moves back once more to particularized physical realities, in a very precise account, in plain language, of the man's happy antics. The prancing about is lively and ordinary but Ray prances "like a tower," and has a rod like Aaron's. After the transformation into "snakes or flames" he sinks on to the grass and debris of the Worm, rendered with wonderfully hard and sharp precision in Thomas's version of what Yeats meant when he wrote, in "At Algeciras—A Meditation Upon Death," about the "substantial joy" of "the actual shells of Rosses' shore."

From this extreme point of the headland, the most westerly point of the Gower peninsula, you see neither Devonshire nor Carmarthenshire, but only sea. (As I suggested in chapter 1, it is a rare occasion when a knowledge of the region supplements what is in the story.) Like Joyce's Gabriel Conroy in "The Dead," and Huckleberry Finn before him, Raymond has gone as far as he can, as he goes west, to find freedom, extremity, land's end, and wildness. And the narrator is there with him.

But it can't last. Holiday and freedom can only be momentary, and time and routine return, in Ray's case to bring back the obsessional story—from which he's been briefly released—of his brother's suffering and death. And this is rendered through the narrator's sympathetic imagination, which doesn't slip easily into listening, or feeling, is indeed reluctant—especially after his taste of the free west—but powerfully compelled by loving friendship, and also by the grip of storytelling. The telling is the more compulsive for being a repetition of what has happened before:

> He drew down into himself, and the rock, to him, became dark and a house with blinds drawn. . . .
>
> I knew what was going to happen by the way Ray lowered his head and brought his shoulders up so that he looked like a man with no neck. . . . He stared at his dusty white shoes and I knew what shapes his imagination made of them; they were the feet of a man dead in bed, and he was going to talk about his brother. Sometimes, leaning against

a fence when we watched football, I caught him staring at his own thin hand; he was thinning it more and more, removing the flesh, seeing Harry's hand in front of him, with the bones appearing through the sensitive skin.

"I knew what shapes his imagination made." It is a painfully convincing and circumstantial imaging of imaginative memory, and its details, like those transformed dirty white shoes and thinned hand, are incisive and unforgettable. It is about being taken out of yourself, but—in a clever turn of the story—not by radiant free nature but by tragic human nature. It may remind us of Keats's famous allegory of imaginative development from the Chamber of Maiden-Thought to approach the dark passages where we feel what Wordsworth in "Tintern Abbey" calls "the burden of the mystery."

Thomas's history of imagination is told in two stages, as the characters move through pastoral joy and freedom, into the recall of everyday pain and dying. In this story Dylan Thomas makes his narrator mourn for a stranger's death, as he comes to understand and pity his friend's horror and grief at that death. It is a story about creative vitality's acceptance of death, and also about condolence. Its shifting and developing emotions are tracked and expressed as a process, and strongly and precisely particularized, without a trace of sentimentality.

It is also one of the best examples I know of imagined imagination, to be placed in a high place, beside the end of Joyce's greatest story, "The Dead." In that conclusion to a story, a volume, and an egocentric illusion, Gabriel Conroy finally moves out of his own preoccupied and other-engrossing imagination, through a painful jealous reluctance, to accept the vision of his wife's memory, which like Ray's obsessed recall in Thomas's story, is also a memory of suffering, death, love and grief. I am not for one minute suggesting that this is a conscious imitation—I think a deliberate use of a paradigm is probably less likely than in the case of *Under Milk Wood*—

but I think it is an equivalent telling, a story written out of deeply felt personal experience, a response to life, but in a way which has been informed and sophisticated by reading another powerful and congenial story, a response to art. And Joyce and Thomas are joined by a strange coincidence: Joyce's story was not only about imagination and mutuality but also about someone remembering a very young man who died from consumption, and in the memory spoiling another's dream of holiday and freedom. "Who Do You Wish Was With Us?" could have been called "The Dead."

Both stories are readable as stories about stories, reflexively and profoundly concerned with the artist's imagination, which can be compelled—in the process Keats brilliantly christened negative capability—to identify with other people's experience and their imagination. But it is also concerned with the acceptance of death, an act which sometimes seems too melodramatic and even facile in Thomas's early morbidity, about which, however, he was capable of joking, as he frequently does in his letters to Pamela Hansford Johnson.

The story of imagination's grasp of death is very unlike Joyce in being all done through implication and particularity. The celebrated conclusion of "The Dead," where Gabriel's bitter spousal experience of what Richard Ellmann, in his discussion in *James Joyce,* calls mutuality, is transformed into that generalized vision of the falling snow, is very different from Thomas's quiet end, with the two friends marooned on the tidal island. A tidal island is a great image for the temporary experience of freedom and, finally, of imaginative acquiescence. But Thomas is like Joyce in taking us from the human to the nonhuman in nature, sea covering Rhossili rocks instead of snow covering Ireland. Thomas even echoes the words of Joyce's last paragraph, "the living and the dead":

Cold came up, spraying out of the sea, and I could make a body for it, icy antlers, a dripping tail, a rippling face with fishes passing across it. A wind, cornering the Head, chilled through our summer shirts, and the sea began to cover our rock quickly, our rock already covered with friends, with living and dead, racing against the darkness. We did not speak as we climbed. I thought: "If we open our mouths we'll both say 'Too late, it's too late.'" We ran over the spring-board grass and the scraping rock needles, down the hollow . . . and along the ragged flat. We stood on the beginning of the Head and looked down, though both of us could have said, without looking: "The sea is in."

The sea was in. The slipping stepping-stones were gone. On the mainland, in the dusk, some little figures beckoned to us. Seven clear figures, jumping and calling. I thought they were the cyclists.

The subdued utterance of the last four brief sentences — the local, almost private reference to the marooned isolation followed by the mention of the cyclists seen earlier — returns us to the ordinary life, modulating from the sonorous, grand Joycean symbolic reference to the matter-of-fact. This conclusion takes us back to the ordinary everyday life which began the story, so realistically, and also marks an implicit and indirect acceptance of death as the common ending.

Just before the recognition of full tide, the sun sets, and just before sunset the title wish has been framed and answered as the narrator asks Ray, "Who do you wish was with us?" trying to lighten the death grief and avert the expected answer by harking back to his cousin Gwilym in "The Peaches," "I wish Gwilym was here, too." At last he gets the emphatic threefold answer, for which the title has prepared us from the start, "I wish my brother was with us. . . . I wish Harry was here. I wish he was here now, at this moment, on this rock."

He is, when the narrator asserts his presence in the Joycean phrase, "our rock already covered with friends, with living and dead." And the last spurt of fanciful creativity, as the narrator makes—or says he can make—a "body" for the cold, is a subdued self-reference to art's assertive and articulative power and final mortal impotence. It is a wonderful story, rising to the Joycean occasion which has instructed it, but asserting its own equally profound and original variation of the life-death theme. Thomas's handling of plain and extravagant narrative, and of plain and extravagant style, make a flexible and sensitive medium. It is his language at its most controlled, as the narrator's imagination has to be controlled: imitative and fresh, empathetic and reflexive, fantastic and realistic, poignantly placing two imaginations in relationship. The affectively dynamic story is constructed, like a lyric, as a rhythmical structure of feeling.

This is a high point in Thomas's narrative power and craft. However flexible, novel, musical, and inventive Thomas's original language appears to us across the genres, in film script, drama, broadcast and lyrical narrative, it is in his poetry, not his prose, that it is sustained, profoundly, strangely, intensely, and brilliantly. My central poetic sample here is one of Thomas's dramatic lyrics, "If my head hurt a hair's foot," a poem which imagines imagination, in ways which are both like and unlike the ways of "Who Do You Wish Was With Us?"

In *A Portrait of the Artist as a Young Man* Stephen Dedalus defines the most primitive lyric stage of literature by using the model of a simple cry. This poem is more elaborate than that, but it turns on two cries, those of an unborn child and its mother. It is an impassioned dialogue between these two cries, the one imaginary, the other familiar, of love and solicitude, but both imagined, and not experienced, by Dylan Thomas as he was expecting his first child. Thomas insisted that this poem was not obscure, and he was right. Here are the first three stanzas in which the unborn child addresses the mother:

"If my head hurt a hair's foot
Pack back the downed bone. If the unpricked ball of my
    breath
Bump on a spout let the bubbles jump out.
Sooner drop with the worm of the ropes round my throat
Than bully ill love in the clouted scene.

All game phrases fit your ring of a cockfight:
I'll comb the snared woods with a glove on a lamp,
Peck, sprint, dance on fountains and duck time
Before I rush in a crouch the ghost with a hammer, air,
Strike light, and bloody a loud room.

If my bunched, monkey coming is cruel
Rage me back to the making house. My hand unravel
When you sew the deep door. The bed is a cross place.
Bend, if my journey ache, direction like an arc or make
A limp and riderless shape to leap nine thinning months."

As a feminist I feel a certain unease about a poem which
might be thought to appropriate a story of pregnancy, and
one which includes a dramatization of the woman's point of
view. But when examining what feels like a historically inevitable judicial response, I recognize its stronger opposite,
an unease about a common male failure to imagine the
woman's fear, pain, courage and love. I have come to admire
the imagination with which sympathy and love are projected
on to the character of the unborn child, and in a way which
wonderfully puts off manhood. In three ways and for three
creative purposes: to impersonate a woman, to impersonate
an unborn child, and to forgo impersonating a gendered
creature.

The imagery is masculine, true, taken from the special jar-
gon of prizefighting, a sport which Thomas, like many men
in South Wales, enjoyed, and cockfighting, which he had
probably only read, or perhaps heard, about. (The editors of

CP have a note explaining that a famous South Welsh boxer, Jimmy Wilde, who was a miner, was known as "the ghost with a hammer in his hand" [p. 231].) The bullying, violent, and physical language serves two purposes. It is appropriate for the imagining of the bloodiness and laboriousness of labor: sensitively apt for someone who had never witnessed childbirth is that image of the suddenness and force of birth, "rush in a crouch." And it deconstructs itself before it starts, "Sooner drop . . . Than bully ill love." Of course it is witty as well as apt, and the child speaks in a father's physical language, a language which is rough, drawn from a liking for men's aggressive sports, sexy, in "cockfight," "unpricked," and "balls," remembering women's things too, in "clouted scene."

The poet imagines a mother who makes it clear that this is a poem truthfully imagining a pregnancy (in the days before the embryo could be sexed). She addresses the unborn child first "as my dear," then as "my daughter or son." (There is a marked contrast with Seamus Heaney's poem about pregnancy, "Act of Union," in which he significantly imagines his child as masculine.) Thomas's poem gains in realism and also in appropriate and touching generalization, because in it (as not in Heaney, where the Irish political allegory needs a militant hero) gender is irrelevant. Perhaps that is putting it too negatively.

The absence of gender is indeed a startling positive. As I said in chapter 1, Heaney—judging what he sees as the complicit Welsh stereotyping in the "delightful" reminiscences and *Milk Wood*—described Thomas's intelligence as insufficiently "wary," and here in a different context, where sex and not race is the issue, the concept of a wary intelligence, and a wary imagination, can be usefully invoked. Thomas is brilliantly wary here, in his total avoidance of sexism. Caitlin Thomas complained that Thomas did not attend the births of his children, and was not strong on early caring for babies and infants, but his parental imagination was attentive, caring, and expansive.

Here he startlingly and lovingly creates a new character, Everychild, out of a new language. If that language is physical and violent, it is stunningly naive. The poem is narrative, but the story is told through drama, in the two individualized and differentiated kinds of speech, though both of course recognizably the poet's style. The old story of gestation and birth is combined with, and made strange by, the novel and particularized story of a child who can fearfully, tenderly, and precisely imagine its birth and the pain for its mother, to be joined by the responsive story of parental loving, protective and heartbreakingly aware of the limits of the care and protection. If Thomas gets into the imagination of the child through the imagination of a father, he gets into the imagination of a mother by the same medium of parental anxiety, tenderness, and wisdom. So the word "appropriation" seems inappropriate: we can see the bridges his imagination moves across, and they are what men and women have in common, before they are born, and before their children are born.

The story is made both old and new, ordinary and grotesquely odd, by the emotional and sensuous image making. The first three lines mime the position and appearance of the embryo and introduce us to the language of Everychild. We read its lexis and its syntax: every word and construction is familiar but none of us—and more relevantly, no other character in Thomas's poetry—would ever say any of the sentences. The language is of course that of the poet's familiar organized music, with its cross-patternings of assonance and alliteration on which he worked so strenuously, and its sparky periphrastic wit, sometimes obvious, like "cockfight," sometimes more subtle, like "game," "ring," and "clouted." The craft is always at the service of the emotional emphasis. The vowel echoes make the sense stresses, for instance in "bunched monkey coming" and "rage me back to the making house." The first phrase makes its weight felt, like some of the bunched-together heavy stresses in Hopkins's sprung rhythms, here urgent, grave, and big. It is dramatic style, because Thomas's strange and punning language seems wonderfully right for an unborn child, an alien, starting to learn and to play.

We hear its naive idiolect rather as we hear Stephen Dedalus in his babbling very good time at the beginning of *A Portrait of the Artist as a Young Man:* "he sang that song. That was his song." But where Joyce uses starkly simple sentences and lisping baby talk, Thomas uses some simple but not infantile sentences, a lot of play, and a kind of metaphorical literalness. Unlike Joyce, who uses the free indirect style, Thomas is using direct speech but with a similar compromise between adult and childish lexis and syntax.

Thomas, lover of strange language, gave a broadcast reading on "The Poetry of Wonder" (TB) and obviously enjoyed imagining surrogate speakers who might be likely to use strange languages, making us wonder and speaking in wonder: the Old Testament Father-God, Christ, young Aesop, Noah, storytelling parents, a madwoman in love with a madman, and here a fetus.

The fetal language has a weird childlike quality, in the playfulness and the simplicity of lexis and syntax, both in literal statement, "The bed is a cross place," and in metaphor, "the deep door." That simplicity is profound, as if the unborn creature needs or hits on metaphor because it has to find its own words for things, for the very first time, physically and pragmatically, avoiding the ordinary language, and especially abstractions and technical terms. So the metaphors avoid expected grown-up speech, and perhaps don't know that they are metaphors, almost appearing like wrong words, though of course the poet and reader know they are right words. One key figure in this fetal style is catachresis, an apparent clash or stupidity, and perfect for the uneducated fetus, who of course knows no better: for instance, the "hair's foot," "the unpricked ball," and "downed bone," which jumble body parts, and confuse the relation of tenor (subject signified) and vehicle (carrier or signifier or illustration) like Milton's catachretic synecdoche "blind mouths" in "Lycidas."

It is a conceptual language too: in "the making house" and "deep door" concepts of creative matrix and a huge entrance are conveyed through simplicity and physicality. They are metaphors which sound like a grasping—an apprehension rather than a comprehension—of sense data, for the first time. The fetus seems to be encountering substances and acts and things, urgently, because there's no time to lose; gravely, because what could be more important than this life and death, this pain and sacrifice and love; with dignity, because it's a ritual, to be encountered or avoided; grotesquely and fantastically, because it's all impossible. The sexual wordplay, like "coming," "pricked," and "ball," are just right for the child's innocence, manipulated by the poet's knowing wit but expressing a kind of blundering ignorance, like that shown by the child Stephen Dedalus as he meditates on the sense and sound of "cock," "suck," and "kiss." And there is a simple amusing physicality, like "bump on a spout." All childish, new, bright and strange.

Dylan Thomas's poetic language is normally strange and original, and here it is heightened in its strangeness and originality, as real baby talk is, commonly making the adults wonder at the oddity and perspicacity of its truly naive and individual encounter with experience. Here of course imitation is mingled with novelty, in trial and error. Everything is being said for the first time—not a bad definition of originality. An interesting comparison can be made with the exotic language of Ted Hughes—a poet strongly influenced by Thomas—in the title poem of his volume *Wodwo*, as Hughes invents an idiolect for a new creature using language as it meets experience for the first time, and existing between categories, as

Thomas's unborn child exists—with a special tenderness for such minimal humanity—without gender. In this instance it is adapted for language imagined at its origins, in a premature, but intelligent, anticipation of Chomsky's deep structure. Unlike baby talk the idiolect is grammatically and syntactically and poetically skillful but it empowers the imagined voice to be fresh and new, amazing us, as birth does, with renewals of creativity.

Some of this we feel the more strongly after a first reading, having taken in the context and contrast of the adult voice. The mother speaks:

"No. Not for Christ's dazzling bed
Or a nacreous sleep among soft particles and charms
My dear would I change my tears or your iron head.
Thrust, my daughter or son, to escape, there is none, none,
    none,
Nor when all the ponderous heaven's host of waters breaks.

Now to awake husked of gestures and my joy like a cave
To the anguish and carrion, to the infant forever unfree,
O my lost love bounced from a good home;
The grain that hurries this way from the rim of the grave
Has a voice and a house, and there and here you must couch
    and cry.

Rest beyond choice in the dust-appointed grain,
At the breast stored with seas. No return
Through the waves of the fat streets nor the skeleton's thin
    ways.
The grave and my calm body are shut to your coming as
    stone,
And the endless beginning of prodigies suffers open."

Though there is a strong sense of labor, in such physical words as "iron," "husked," and "bounced," the mother is given a noticeably more abstract language than the fetus, with latinate, and even scientific, words, like "nacreous," "particles," "ponderous," and "prodigies," religious metaphors, "dazzling bed," "host of waters," and "dust-appointed," and obscure or paradoxical images, "joy like a cave," "grain that hurries," "breast stored with seas," "fat street," "endless beginning." None of these words or phrases is impenetrable but they all need to be unriddled, unlike the images of the unborn's speech, which are extraordinary but always clear.

The poem tells the old story of birth and death, together with Thomas's obsessional story, told from start to finish of his career, of birth into death. The stories are made new not only by the words but by the whole idea of the child born to die but made alive by fierce human love, a child longing to spare its mother, the mother knowing she cannot spare the child, but speaking with the strength of the life force, defiant about pain, and experiencing a mother's joy, honestly and rationally, as "a cave" containing anguish and carrion, in a vivid and apt revision of Plato's cave of being.

(The poem, its theme, and the cave imagery, are recalled, consciously or unconsciously, by Sylvia Plath, another poet influenced by Thomas, in her poem about mother love's warm protectiveness and its terribly acknowledged limits, "Nick and the Candlestick.")

This poem is narrative subdued to lyric, powerfully making a contrast but also a continuity of strong feeling, and made dramatic as it adapts the language congenial to the poet, imagining a language right for these characters and this relationship, abstracted but passionate and thinking creatures fantastically projected in a dynamic dialogue. It is most concentrated in this poetry, but across all his genres, the original language sounds.

4. The Reflexive Poet

The Theme of Art

Under Milk Wood has few moments of reflexive awareness, befitting its simplicity of concept, dialogue, and character, but the play for voices presents itself from the outset as
artifice, the uncharacterized narrators directly and constantly
addressing their sightless audience with "Listen" and "Hush"
and "Look." There is detailed description, dramatically addressed to the listeners, "You can hear the dew falling, and
the hushed down breathing. Only your eyes are unclosed, to
see the black and folded town fast, and slow, asleep" (p. 2).
There is narration, "Sinbad Sailors, over the taproom of the
Sailors Arms, hugs his damp pillow whose secret name is
Gossamer Beynon" (p. 18). There is the comic dry science of
its Voice of a Guide Book, in strong contrast with the warm
natural piety of the nearest—but distant—representation of
an author's voice, that of the simple poet and writer of the
White Book of Llaregyb, the Reverend Eli Jenkins.

He is said to be dreaming of *eisteddfodau* and planning intricate rhymes, but his powers are illustrated in his two excellently prayerful simple poems, one for the beginning and
the other for the end of the day. They are rich in English and
Welsh place-names, and in some ways reminiscent of that
other South Welsh poet, W. H. Davies, admired by Thomas
with reservations, whose poem, "Can I forget the sweet days
that have been," is not unlike the writing of Eli Jenkins,
though with a less hymnlike form and feeling. The Reverend
Eli Jenkins is a benign joke in his simplicities, almost—but I
stress almost—as far removed from the real author as you

could get: he shares his author's feeling for nature, which sings within his singing, and he is a local poet:

> A tiny dingle is Milk Wood
> By Golden Grove 'neath Grongar,
> But let me choose and oh! I should
> Love all my life and longer

> To stroll among our trees and stray
> In Goosegog Lane, on Donkey Down,
> And hear the Dewi sing all day,
> And never, never leave the town.
> (p. 25)

There is a gentle reflexive joke at the heart of the poetic comedy about traditional religion and the new poetry, because in this Welsh town that never was and never could be, the poet is the preacher, his faith a naive Christian version of Thomas's affirmations and place loyalties, his poetry simple in content and form. Simple faith and simple poetry are placed and praised, but without sentimentality or romantic idealism, because their limits are recognized in affectionate pastiche, and recognize their opposite, the alien modernist skilled in artifice and given to complexities of belief and art.

While the play's exclusion of the explicitly sophisticated comments and literary suggestions found in *Portrait of the Artist as a Young Dog* points to the triumph of its unassuming negative capability, it points also to the play's extreme simplifications and its larger exclusions. The complications of tragedy, for instance, are not even allowed to cast a faint shadow, as they always are in Shakespearean comedy, with the exception of the shadow of death.

Adultery, illegitimacy, drunkenness, jealousy, religious narrowness, and domestic oppression are present, but uncomplicated, made sweet and easy. Gossamer Beynon echoes Cleopatra, but is not Cleopatra; she is less tragic and less political. Polly Garter is a liberated lone parent, but clearly a man's creation, a woman bent on pleasure, and romantic too, promiscuous but memorializing Little Willie Wee in enchanting and amusing erotic song, faithful to him in her fashion. I'm not at all sure that *Under Milk Wood* is "unsentimental revelation," which is what Thomas once said poetry was. It is more like sentimental revelation. But its sentimentality is not crude or naive or unmediated: it is a humorous, sexy, and lyrical sentimentality, seasoned by its playfully mannered original language, its narrative norm distinguished from the gently characterized and parodic style of the Reverend Jenkins's inset verses, those poems artlessly, but artfully, placed within the play.

The stories and poems are, in many ways, complexly aware of imagination and art. If Dylan Thomas is with the great modernists in his subversive forms, he is so most centrally and conspicuously in his artistic self-consciousness, in what we have come to call reflexivity, designating its extreme formal and thematic dominations as postmodernist. One of the most impressive features of his poetry, and of the fiction at its best, is the double vision involved in such insistent self-awareness. It is never a merely introspective or, worse, a fashionable act or gesture, but stands with the self-consciousness of Chaucer and Shakespeare, as a life awareness as well as an art awareness. When he writes about imagination, implicitly or explicitly, it is always—or almost always—about what Coleridge calls the Primary Imagination,[1] which we all share as we try to order, unify, idealize, and remake our lives, to withdraw as we project mind and feeling into lives outside our own.

The act of withdrawal and projection is clear in the short story I have already discussed, "Who Do You Wish Was With Us?" where the unwilling, willing, able and loving imagining by the narrator of his friend's story, and his friend's unwilling, willing, able and loving imagining of the brother's story, stand in their strong doubling for human love and for the artist's imaginative storytelling. What is true of this story is true to some extent of others in the collection, and runs as a strong thematic concern which makes the book a portrait of a young artist in the making. But because it is a book made by, and is to some extent about, the imaginative power of memory, it constantly shifts its center from the imagining of the teller to the other characters who often play the most active part in the story. The first person can be forced out of self-occupation, to observe, and then to become, a third person. Some of the stories incorporate a clear analytic awareness of what is happening, a sense of self-pride turning to empathy; the relationship of what Keats called the egotistical or Wordsworthian sublime to what he called the negative capability of the Shakespearean, or chameleon, poet.

There are stories in which the narrator is wonderfully withdrawn and self-abnegating, leaving the creativity to the characters, as he does gloriously in "A Visit to Grandpa's," where the narrating boy is creative in his dreams, where a manic inventiveness claims kinship with and even seems to take inspiration from, the cunning mad fantasies of his fast-riding grandfather.

But most of the stories concentrate subtly but conspicuously on the narrator's imagination. In "The Peaches," for example, the story attributes a large measure of creative awareness to the little boy in the remembered past. His arrival at the farm, after a journey in which he has been left outside in the cold while his uncle drinks in the pub, is made the occasion for the sense of a central self, warm, protected, secure, and inspired. The young artist's creative pride is placed in a simple, yet not so simple, human context, as it is intertwined with a child's transformative fear of the life glimpsed through the window, a fear born from cold solitude and the rough unknown adult world of pub life:

The passage grew dark too suddenly, the walls crowded in, and the roofs crouched down. To me, staring timidly there in the dark passage in a strange town, the swarthy man appeared like a giant in a cage surrounded by clouds, and the bald old man withered into a black hump with a white top; two white hands darted out of the corner with invisible cards. A man with spring-heeled boots and a two-edged knife might be bouncing towards me from Union Street.

Solitude is consoled, then fear enlarged, by a romantic imagination which has been enriched—like that of Joyce's narrating boy in *A Portrait of the Artist as a Young Man*—by reading:

> I was cut off from the night by a stained square. A story I had made in the warm, safe island of my bed, with sleepy midnight Swansea flowing and rolling round outside the house, came blowing down to me then with a noise on the cobbles. I remembered the demon in the story, with his wing and hooks, who clung like a bat to my hair as I battled up and down Wales after a tall, wise, golden girl from Swansea convent.

When the pub door opens the child's story is "burned" up. Then as he arrives at the farm, art and life are again drawn together indissolubly as he feels the security of the warm kitchen, and all the fêting and fussing he gets from the loving aunt who greets him as a royal nephew from the town: "I stood among the shining and striking like a prince taking off his disguise. . . . One minute I was small and cold . . . a snub-nosed storyteller lost in his own adventures . . . the next I was a royal nephew . . . standing in the snug centre of my stories." He enjoys a sense of safety and confident control, in contrast with the doubt, anxiety, alienation, and fear he felt in the pub yard, though those disturbing emotions come to be placed as experience past and remembered, and not wholly negative or entirely unenjoyable.

Thomas uses the adult viewpoint, which sees and renders what the child could not see, or saw without understanding, as he listens or peeps through the window of the pub, or later overhears in snatches when his aunt remonstrates with his uncle about his drinking and profligacy, and laments the shameful visit of Mrs. Williams, the snobbish rich woman who rejects the tinned peaches and takes her complaining son, a paying guest, back home. The full adult story of the farm's poverty, the drinking brutal desperate feckless uncle, the hard-driven desperate woman, and the repressed half-crazy religious son, is a subtext not fully understood or expressed by the narrator, allowed to make a piecemeal but recurring appearance the more powerful for being ironically held back and held down.

Dylan, as the narrator is named in this story, is a sharp observer and a gifted teller. He is like many heroes and heroines, authors' favorites who sometimes become professional tellers, like David Copperfield, Proust's Marcel, and who are sometimes talented amateurs, like Jane Eyre, Maggie Tulliver, and Alan Sillitoe's Arthur Seaton in *Saturday Night and Sunday Morning*.

In a mock-confession game Dylan privately summarizes the tall boastful tales of his wickedness:

I stole from Gwyneth's bag; I stole twelve books in three visits to the library and threw them away in the park; I drank a cup of my water to see what it tasted like; I beat a dog with a stick so that it would lick my hand.

He first refused to tell his stories in public, then later in a joint confessional with Jack narrates with embellishments, "I killed a man once. . . . Honest to Christ, I shot him through the heart." Jack is provoked to tell his rival tales of wickedness, then to tell tales in a letter home which leads to his disdainful exit from the poor farm.

The narrator's childhood creativity is marked by a feeling

of enjoyable centrality and power, common to several stories in the volume, and by a particularly enthusiastic recognition of happy play and exultant physicality:

I felt all my young body like an excited animal surrounding me, the torn knees bent, the bumping heart, the long heat and depth between the legs, the sweat prickling in the hands, the tunnels down to the eardrums, the little balls of dirt between the toes, the eyes in the sockets, the tucked-up voice, the blood racing, the memory around and within flying, jumping, swimming, and waiting to pounce. There, playing Indians in the evening, I was aware of myself in the exact centre of a living story, and my body was my adventure and my name.

Seldom has the physical excitement of inventive play been so closely and sharply rendered. The awareness of his body makes a link between the stories and the poems, but here it is rendered in simple, straightforward, particularized detail. Such particularity plays a substantiating role in his amusing and affectionate portrait of the artist as a young dog, at play. "Like an excited animal surrounding me": at first sight simple, but astonishing, unique, accurate, and many-meaninged. The pleasure and fun also express an important insight, like that in Wordsworth's visionary poem about childhood creativity and the natural habitat, the "Ode: Intimations of Immortality from Recollections of Early Childhood." Wordsworth gravely insists that such imitative, sung, and spoken play is an important part of imaginative growth:

See, at his feet, some little plan or chart,
Some fragment from his dream of human life,
Shaped by himself with newly-learned art;
A wedding or a festival
A mourning or a funeral,
    And this hath now his heart,

And unto this he frames his song;
   Then will he fit his tongue
To dialogues of business, love, or strife.

This emphasis is to recur in Thomas's poems, and it is especially prominent in "Fern Hill," which comes very close to the Immortality Ode in sensation, thought and feeling.

Other characters in "The Peaches" also enjoy the excitement, indulgence and free play of telling, especially the eloquent cousin Gwilym, whose expert—but not only—genre is the sermon. He puts on a great performance for Dylan and Jack on the dusty wagon in the barn, his preaching presented as a comic but sympathetic imitation, rather than a parody, of the Welsh nonconformist genre. The artist's attentiveness to emotional trajectory is assimilated to the child's feeling with apparent ease:

> I sat on the hay and stared at Gwilym preaching, and heard his voice rise and crack and sink to a whisper and break into singing and Welsh and ring triumphantly and be wild and meek. The sun, through a hole, shone on his praying shoulders, and he said: "O God, thou art everywhere all the time, in the dew of the morning, in the frost of the evening, in the field and the town, in the preacher and the sinner, in the sparrow and the big buzzard. Thou canst see everything, right down deep in our hearts; Thou canst see us when the sun is gone; Thou canst see us when there aren't any stars, in the gravy blackness, in the deep, deep, deep, deep pit; Thou canst see and spy and watch us all the time, in the little black corners, in the big cowboys' prairies. . . . O God, mun, you're like a bloody cat."

It is noticeable that Gwilym's inventive witty succinct style —"gravy blackness"—and his solemn pantheism closely resemble two striking features of Thomas's work. The preacher is wonderfully characterized, especially in that "wild and meek." Gwilym is a good storyteller as well as a preacher, and in a clever psychological and sociological stroke the hellfire preacher is also made to specialize in melodramatic brief anecdotes about sex and violence. These are as vivid and as funny as his apostrophes to God:

> He told me stories about girls who died for love. "And she put a rope round the tree but it was too short," he said; "she stuck a penknife in her bosoms but it was too blunt." . . . "She jumped in the cold river, she jumped," he said, his mouth against my ear, "arse over tip and Diu, she was dead." He squeaked like a bat.

So the farm has its creativity, outside Dylan, who is like Joyce's nameless child whose viewpoint is central in some early stories in *Dubliners*, "Araby," "The Sisters," and "An Encounter." The fictitious Dylan gathers memories of innocent impressions, some of which, like Joyce's boy, he perceives as obscure images, sharply perceived but not understood: for instance, he sees Gwilym in the lavatory "moving his hands" as he reads some book. Indeed, the more diffused pictures of the poverty, hardship, and deterioration of what he much later came to call "the insanitary farm," is presented from a double viewpoint, yielding the kind of implicit social commentary congenial to Thomas's undidactic genius. We see how the child's blurred, discrete, and often comic fragments of story have yielded their meanings over the years, though those meanings are tactfully left for a reader's inference to work on, and not summarized and articulated by the explicating adult.

"The Peaches," as the first story in the book, sets the narrative pattern of doubled point of view and implicit meaning. All the other stories contain a creative narrator who is both teller and listener, retelling somebody else's story. Sometimes his creativity is subdued, not emphasized as particularly creative but naturalized as the ordinary fantasy and play of the imaginative child, as in "Patricia, Edith, and Arnold," where the narrator is at his youngest. He is presented as dividing his attention between observation and play, adding a new example to the important play imagery in Thomas's artistic self-analysis, but his imagination is much less prominently inspected than the boy's in "The Peaches." However, it is given the responsibility of beginning the third-person narrative story, "the small boy in his invisible engine, the Cwmdonkin special. . . . he backed the Flying Welshman from the washhouse to the open door of the coalhole." "He" is the sharp but not wholly comprehending recorder and teller, fascinated by the tragicomic love triangle and its dénouement in a snowy Cwmdonkin Park, staged in the shelter by the bowling green. (The actual park shelter was indeed a rendezvous for children and lovers, later replaced by a much uglier structure.)

The child actually plays a partly innocent, partly mischievous role as a telltale in the story, but his prime role is that of spectator. He is gathering material for memory to store and imagination to retrieve, but his powers of observation, memory, and reassembly are left to speak for themselves. As the central narrating character grows older, his powers grow; as the inset narratives accumulate throughout the volume, the portrait is filled in. It is all done implicitly, but the artist's imagination is never explicitly assessed as it is in Dickens's *David Copperfield* or Joyce's *Portrait of the Artist*, for instance, where the same powers are dramatized in the child, shown to develop in the adult teller, and emphasized, judged, and analyzed.

In "Just Like Little Dogs" the narrator is the quiet night-walker who joins the two sad mismarried husbands under the railway arch by the Swansea sands, in the rain, listening to their odd story. Here he is explicitly presented as a listener, but a sharply receptive one, joining in the telling of the story within the story, images of his receptivity enriching the bald telling. His receptivity is shown as he observes and curiously questions, "Why was the soft-faced young man with his tame devil's eyebrows, standing like a stone figure with a glow-worm in it? he should have a nice girl to bully him gently." As Tom begins to tell his story, he imagines "a new stranger walking on the sands past and hearing all of a sudden that high voice out of a hole . . . listening in a panic." As he listens he visualizes the narrative, "he described her. I saw her clearly. . . . I saw her ambling solidly along the sands . . . her plump, kind face." Towards the end, narrative seems to give way to total identification, time and place dissolving, "The storytelling thing in the arch gave way to the loving night in the dunes. . . . The arch was as high as the sky. I lay like a pimp in a bush by Tom's side."

The random flow of response is excellently and curtly done, as in the explicit comment that in his solitude and night walks the narrator-listener takes on the life outside himself. Here as in "Old Garbo" and "One Warm Saturday," the town is a creative matrix, the seat of imagination:

I was a lonely nightwalker and a steady stander-on-corners. . . . I liked to walk through the wet town after midnight. . . . I never felt more a part of the remote and overpressing world, or more full of arrogance and pity, and humanity, not for myself alone, but for the unfeeling systems in the upper air, Mars and Venus and Brazell and Skully, men in China and St. Thomas, scorning girls and ready girls . . . unapproachable women out of the fashion magazines, seven feet high, sailing slowly in their flat, glazed creations.

In such commentary the solemnity of the subject is lightened and brightened by his startling juxtapositions, and his sallies of exaggeration and fantasy: the local and the cosmic, the sublime and the squalid, are brought together.

There are two stories which seem straightforwardly autobiographical and are explicitly concerned with literary invention, "The Fight," about the narrator's (and Dylan Thomas's) meeting with Dan (Daniel Jones, friend, writer, scholar, and composer), another gifted boy, writer and musician, with whom he shares creativity and talk about creativity; and "Where Tawe Flows," where he describes the political and literary discussions of characters based on some actual Swansea friendships. Mr. Thomas is the writer to be, and the quoted writings directly dramatize a funny and touching story of an aspiring writers' group, like Gwilym's sermon, too sympathetic to be called parody, though comically placing the limits and limitations of texts and contexts. "The Fight," like some of the broadcasts, moves outside the autobiographical center with the marvelously dotty anecdote of a woman visitor who has threatened suicide and is deliciously goaded by the boys trying and dying for a repeat.

Both stories are remarkable for doing that rare thing, including (actual) examples of the artist-character's early poetry and prose, produced in good-tempered unambiguous self-mockery. (Joyce did this, more equivocally, with his villanelle in *Portrait of the Artist.*) The artistic specimens illustrate creativity, and at the same time make high-spirited fun, in a Walter Mitty drama in which the narrator imagines himself as the great surgeon, the great lover, and the great writer. But these two overt portraits of the artist, amusing though they are, not least in their self-criticism of ambition and high-flying poetry, are less subtly concerned with creativity than stories like "The Peaches" which apparently marginalize or subdue the theme of art, but indirectly say profound things about it. Thomas's portraits of the artist are at their best when working through indirection and subtext, like Yeats's fishing crane who may catch a trout if he can manage not to show that he wants to.

There is another partly autobiographical story about Thomas's experience on the *South Wales Evening Post* as a trainee reporter, "Old Garbo." It is a strikingly understated compressed piece of reporting, set in the seedy pubs of the docks, with a heroine — Old Garbo — whose comitragedy, vividly narrated at second hand by the choric gossip of a pub, is the key example of the sad squalid life milling round the young artist. Inspired to create "this story," he shows it to Mr. Farr, the senior reporter, is corrected and rebuked for getting the details wrong, and led to vow, famously, "I'll put them all in a story by and by." This is most simply a story about itself, but also manages to make heartbreak and squalor comic and tragic.

He put some of the town's inhabitants into the last story in the book (the third in order of composition), "One Warm Saturday," which has been much discussed, and praised as the best story in the volume. It is in some ways the most ambitious story, the one most explicitly concerned with creativity, and as I suggested when discussing "Who Do You Wish Was With Us?" complementary to that story. Both stories are concerned to dramatize, and implicitly appraise, an imaginative displacement of the central observer and narrator.

In "Who Do You Wish Was With Us?" the displacement silently demonstrates the teller's potential as an imaginative artist. By imagining, projecting, and annihilating the self, Keats-like, he can hear and tell other people's stories as well as his own. In "One Warm Saturday," the narrator is at first detached, then located at the very center of his story, then loses creative control in chaos and nightmare. It is the story of imaginative nightmare, danger, chaos, and loss of power. In "Who Do You Wish Was with Us?" the submission of self and loss of control positively transport and transform the imagination. Both are excellent stories, and also understated, central, and profound imaginings of imagination.

In "One Warm Saturday" the chief character at the center of the telling, first shown as a would-be writer at a loose end, dramatizes himself: "he thought dramatically . . . outside all holiday, like a young man doomed forever to the company of his maggots" and

He thought: Poets live and walk with their poems; a man with visions needs no other company. . . . But he was not a poet living and walking, he was a young man . . . with two pounds to spend. . . . he had no visions.

In *The Prose Writing of Dylan Thomas* Linden Peach tells us the central character's name is Jack,[2] but it is important that Jack is only the name Lou suddenly uses, evidently to pretend they aren't strangers, and the narrator always scrupulously calls him "the young man," not breaking the continuity of narrative viewpoint of the whole collection which is occupied either by a character named as Dylan or Mr. Thomas, or, as here, an unnamed character sharing Dylan's and Mr. Thomas's fictionalized characteristics. Namelessness can be risked in the final story, when the reader has learned the name of the game and its chief player.

Like the creative listener in "Just Like Little Dogs," this young man experiences the feelings of imaginative, self-generative, process. But his creative experience is unnerving, a bad trip. He moves from a sense of safe detachment and self-possession to be possessed by the life outside, very much as Keats in a crowded room experienced the annihilation of his central self as identities of people pressed in on him. Thomas uses the Keatsian image of exterior pressure in his brilliant account of creative *Einempfindung* ("perceiving into," a more precise word for imaginative identification than "empathy" because of its image of discovery). There are hints that the possession by the outside world may be more than he bargains for:

> In the safe centre of his own identity, the familiar world about him like another flesh, he sat sad and content in the plain room of the undistinguished hotel at the sea-end of the shabby, spreading town in which everything was happening. He had no need of the dark interior world when Tawe pressed in upon him and the eccentric, ordinary

people came bursting and crawling, with noise and colours, out of their houses . . . the shining shops and the blaspheming chapels, out of the common, wild intelligence of the town.

Taken over by the pressing exteriority, he suffers first extravagant love, then an unexpected nightmare experience of loss. He loses the place and people of his story, going out drunkenly into the chaos of the ruined tenement in a confused exit which takes his imagination, and the story of his imagination, into a surreal mode. Thomas is good at using a slight touch of fantasy in a realistic story, and here there is a weird coincidence—or more than coincidence—which tilts the real into the surreal. The narrator in his alienation and panic experiences a repetition, in the outside world, of events and words which he imagined, in Lou's room: he fantasized a *Liebestod* in which he and Lou "imitate the dead," leaving the others to search for them and shout

to them down the dizzy stairs or rummage in the silence about the narrow, obstructed corridors or stumble out into the night to search for them among the cranes and ladders in the desolation of the destroyed houses.

This imagined flight turns out to have been a frightening creative fiat for what he actually experiences when he gets lost. The search and stumbling are his. His speech echoes the exact words he imagined for Lou's protector, Mr. O'Brien: "Lou, where are you? Answer! answer!" which come from his own mouth: "'Lou, where are you?' he cried, 'Answer! Answer!'" His indulgent, extravagant and tipsy love vision becomes the disorienting, extravagant and surreal nightmare of alienation, as dislocations of time and place blending in a confused strangeness. The love story's squalor and speed is set in the context of his romantic aspiration and unsettling vision. E. M. Forster's narrator in *A Passage to India* warned the reader against visions, and this one is a frightening vastation. The mock-heroic visionary artist who enjoyed his wish-fulfilling fantasy is displaced as the plot, eerily taking a hint from his imagination, shows him losing control, and the story drifts into a nightmare fantasy of chaos, loss and alienation, leaving hero and reader doubtful of modes and meanings. The nightmare experience of uncertainty and nightmare's invasion of reality is unnervingly done.

But at the very end there is an expansive move out of the nightmare, as the narrator laments "the small . . . people of the dirty town" who "had lived and loved and died and, always, lost." This conclusion seems to me to be sentimental because it doesn't precisely respond to the story it concludes, modulating into a larger general appeal than the narrative particulars demand. True, the story shows us squalor, poverty, slums, prostitution, pimps, and a dockyard wasteland, the drunken depression of South Wales, but the fantastic episodes do not really form a story of the tragic little people of the town, like "The Peaches," "Patricia, Edith, and Arnold," "Old Garbo," and "Just Like Little Dogs," which concentrate on the rural poor, servants, the sailors and tarts of squalid dockside pubs, and sad layabout mismarried men. They are given as much prominence as the narrator, but the story of "One Warm Saturday" is a portrait of the artist, his amorous vision and drunken hallucination. Although the town's "wild intelligence" is mentioned, its down-and-out characters are less dominant than the imaginative poet through whose mind they are phantasmagorically filtered. There are individual portraits of deadbeat characters, the tarty Lou, her seedy protector, her friend, and the publican, but they aren't presented so much as tragic townspeople as figures in the poet's dream. The scenes on sordid Swansea sands and in Victoria park on a Bank Holiday make a good setting for the narrator's idling amorous imagination, and frighteningly dissolve in a dockland Walpurgisnacht for a Welsh Faust, a Bedlam for a Welsh

Rake. But what Thomas seems to be doing is to write a conclusion more appropriate for the book as a whole, than for this particular story. In the process the marvelous squalid story is a little betrayed, at its end.

A late story, "The Followers," published in *World Review* in 1952 and reprinted in *A Prospect of the Sea* (1955)[3] and *Dylan Thomas: Collected Stories* (1983), also brings together the fantastic and naturalistic modes of Thomas's storytelling, and like "One Warm Saturday" turns on an uncanny coincidence. In it too creativity makes a sly clandestine appearance and takes an eerie shape, as the followers of the title do their following but turn out to be followed.

The story begins with the familiar small town pair, a young-old unnamed first-person narrator and his friend Leslie, empty-pocketed, bored, and at a loose end, having a drink in an empty pub, and then, according to their custom, following a girl home through familiar mean streets. They end up staring and eavesdropping through a back window, as the girl and her mother chat, eat, and look at the family photograph album. Then comes the compounded shock as their reminiscences of dead relatives turn the slice of Swansea life into a ghost story, startling watchers and readers with its ghost as the dead Aunt Katinka suddenly speaks, and speaks of seeing the two Peeping Toms.

The first shock is Katinka's "new" voice, introduced with extreme matter-of-factness, the second the hindsight realization that in a weird way the boys seem to have initiated the ghost. They began to invent the story but let it get out of control, their clandestine act of voyeurism bringing about a scary nemesis which dismisses them from the scene and us from the story. The story is another dangerous creative history with a taint of corruption, observation and curiosity becoming inventive and getting out of hand, as it generates more than it bargains for. After deploring the boring slices of life observed in their voyeuristic following and observing, the idle young men have imagined an exciting life for the girl, "You never know. Perhaps she lives in a huge house with all her sisters" (CS, p. 333), continuing with a fantasy of feathers and a bath, and giving names to the girl and her mother, Hermione and Hetty. All the speculation and invention seem to confer on them a creative responsibility for what happens, and as the final action unfolds they have a sense of preknowledge: "'there's something funny going to happen,' I whispered," and "'It's going to begin,' said Leslie" (CS, p. 335), and "We knew that she and Hermione were only waiting." "And we knew, by their secret smiles that this was what they had been waiting for" (CS, p. 336). But what happens goes beyond their expectations and certainties, as when a story consciously begun sweeps the author or the teller beyond conscious control, in "One Warm Saturday" and "Just Like Little Dogs."

The ghost story can, and probably should, be interpreted in two ways: as an everyday story of ordinary people which has turned out to be much more exciting and frightening than they bargained for, but also as an example of the dangerous power of imagination. The creative act is shown to be hubristic, ineptly egocentric, and also terrifying, as it is in the more sophisticatedly analytic big city story "The Jolly Corner," by Henry James, which is also about the creative fiat and its unexpected revelatory power, and which this tale of provincial life in some ways resembles:

> "Remember that day in Aberystwyth, Katinka?" . . .
> "I wore my new white dress," a new voice said.
> Leslie clutched my hand. (CS, p. 125)

The new voice, a ghost's voice, cuts straight from reminiscence into confrontation: "'You look like a queen, Katinka,' he said, Why are those two boys looking in at the window?" (CS, p. 125). Even the title is revised: who is following whom? (The fear at the end is not unlike the fear at the end of Hitchcock's *Rear Window*, where voyeurism gets a comeuppance.)

The story manages to sustain its comedy, even as its climax jumps out to cry "Boo" at characters and readers. It is that rare thing, a comic ghost story, and Thomas's light touch creates a generative self-analyzing model which is amusing, surprising and frightening, another story which may really be said, like "One Warm Saturday" and "Who Do You Wish Was With Us?" to be about itself.

The poetry too is frequently about itself, and about its genres. It is everywhere aware of its art, and the old and new modes of art. It imagines imagination, in the abstract and in individually and variously reflexive forms. It invents storytellers and poets, natural and supernatural, sane, mad, professional and amateur. It is aware of images, words, and metaphors, and frequently discusses language.

The poetry occasionally discusses itself in a direct and explicit way, as in a poem from *18 Poems*, "Especially when the October wind," which shows simply and clearly that the poet is experiencing things as words and things at the same time:

Of many a thorny shire tell you notes,
Some let me make you of the water's speeches.

This is a specimen stanza from the light simple poem, and it plays gently with the community of words, imagining the talk and shout of distant walkers and players, picking up the tree metaphor to talk about real trees, joking about the oddity of the names we give them: all the *e*s in "beeches" recall the other-vowelled beach, three kinds of roots are noted, the simplicity of a new conceit describes the much-metaphored sound of water in "speeches."

The park is there again in the more complex poem about language, "Once it was the colour of saying," interpreted by Vernon Watkins to be about a conversion from an early obscure symbol-charged style to a more empathetic humane concern. He compares the poem to Yeats's "A Coat," which records the decision to put off a coat "Covered with embroideries / Out of old mythologies" and enterprisingly "walk naked."[4] I think it is even more like George Herbert's "The Forerunners," in which a poet painfully resolves to give up the indulgent love of "Lovely enchanting language" and a "broider'd coat" for the bleak paleness "of a God-devoted poetry."

Thomas's speaker says his writing was about "the colour of saying" and decides

> The gentle seaslides of saying I must undo
> That all the charmingly drowned arise to cockcrow and
>   kill.
> When I whistled with mitching boys through a reservoir
>   park
> Where at night we stoned the cold and cuckoo
> Lovers in the dirt of their leafy beds.

He will write about the past, and its people. The poem goes on to conclude that this future saying will be sympathetic, and will cause him pain:

> The shade of their trees was a word of many shades
> And a lamp of lightning for the poor in the dark;
> Now my saying shall be my undoing,
> And every stone I wind off like a reel.

What is impressive, especially if we compare the poem with "Especially when the October wind," is its powerful indirection. Odd to describe the preoccupation with style as the "colour of saying" saturating his desk, color becoming ink, amusing and precise. Neat to use seaside images both for the ease of that early saying, "gentle seaslides," and then make the romanticized dead "charmingly drowned," rise nastily to "cockcrow and kill."

I don't find Vernon Watkins's interpretation wholly convincing, if we apply it to the whole of Thomas's writing, though it works perfectly well for the change from the surreal and abstract early stories to the stories about real Swansea and Carmarthen life, with which Watkins is chiefly concerned. His interpretation works much less well for the poetry, which continued to be decorative, and which had always had some humanity, as research into the poet's notebooks showed (NP). The poem records a move from the pleasure principle to the experience of imaginative suffering, borne out by many of the stories and some of the poems, and excellently imaged in the word "stone," which is picked up from the stones the bad boys aim at the lovers, to image his own undoing and new doing. He is saying what Virgil made Aeneas say to Dido, that he is compelled to remember pain, to tell the heartbreaking story of his own heartbreak, which is incompatible with sensuous self-indulgence.

A somewhat atypical good poem about writing is

On no work of words now for three lean months in the
  bloody
Belly of the rich year and the big purse of my body
I bitterly take to task my poverty and craft.

This uses economic and political imagery which is so strong that the poem almost becomes a poem about poverty as well as craft, and the impression of a double theme looks like a consequence of a misjudged choice of vehicle for tenor. That tenor is artistic sterility, and the poem is about not being able to write poetry, like Coleridge's "Dejection. An Ode" and Yeats's "The Circus Animals' Desertion." In the first stanza the vehicle is the contemporary subject of unemployment, and its sheer political urgency, with its energy of expression, makes it transform—or threaten to transform—what is secondary and illustrative into what is primary and illustrated. (Another example of this kind of political-personal imbalance is the film *Hiroshima Mon Amour* where the sheer weight of political gravity in the symbolism of atomic war overwhelmed and embarrassed the amorous subject matter.) This poem was published, like "Once it was the colour," in *The Map of Love* (1938), and the impropriety of taste, if we sense it, is almost made up for by the best line, "The lovely gift of the gab bangs back on a blind shaft," which shows that he can be ironic about volubility, and redeemed by an expansion at the end:

> To surrender now is to pay the expensive ogre twice.
> Ancient woods of my blood, dash down to the nut of the
>   seas
> If I take to burn or return this world which is each man's
>   work.

It is in some ways—and in some lines, for instance the first in this stanza, which could have been Auden's—unlike Thomas, and an interesting poem, one of the rare ones which was fully explicated by Thomas, because of that obscure metaphor, "nut of the seas," for which Vernon Watkins demanded an explanation. Thomas explained that "nut" meant origin or source, and said that the far-from-lucid conclusion of the poem meant that he felt he had to do something other than burn or simply return the gifted life (CL, p. 396). The expansion of work into that final sense of planetary responsibility in no way undermines, but rather strengthens, the poem's politics.

In most of his reflexive poetry he is dealing with more than an *ars poetica*. He is exploring an awareness of imaginative art and of imaginative life that is larger than art, as in another of the poems which offers a central portrait of the artist, the "Prologue," already mentioned in chapter 1. Though this poem was written instead of the formal prose self-commentary he had promised his publishers, and found impossible to write, it tells us less about the artist's art than about his themes, especially his celebration of the natural world, beautifully and brilliantly teeming with life. Its intricate but inconspicuous form is amusingly appropriate, a kind of modest masterdemonstration of craft, and the actual self-reference is apparently put in with the lightest touch.

There is a formal process of internal revision, often making a parenthesis of not-too-serious self-correction and criticism, a little like that in "After the funeral," but less complex. Thomas modestly puts himself down but draws attention to his arduous craft, aptly in this poem with its ark-building conceit. When he makes the traditional invocation of bird-song so common in romantic poetry, it is neatly assimilated to the Noah's ark story. At first the image of song is muted, part of a dignified but modest address to the readers he does not know, suitable for a prologue:

> At poor peace I sing
> To you, strangers (though song
> Is a burning and crested act,
> The fire of birds in
> The world's turning wood,
> For my sawn, splay sounds),
> Out of these seathumbed leaves.

Here and throughout the poem, the puns are quietly directing us to nature and art, "seathumbed leaves" and later on "my / Hubbub and fiddle." The speaker goes on to rhapsodize loudly and excitably about building his "bellowing ark," "I, a spinning man, / Glory also this star," and "Hark: I trumpet this place," presenting himself, like Noah, as an amateur builder "as I hack / This rumpus of shapes." The modest but effusive poem of urgent celebration is punctuated, steadied, and cooled by these occasional self-references, lighthearted and self-deprecating, "my hubbub and fiddle, this tune / On a tongued puffball" and "my patch / Work ark." The biblical and responsible creator is comic, as he is in some of the morality plays, and the story of his amateur carpentry allows the modest poet to use his gift of the gab in an appropriate flood of language while controlling and slyly playing down what might seem, or be, an excess of boastful praise and enthusiasm for his craft and art.

In a different mode, "The force that through the green fuse," short but a big poem, is equally concerned with an insistence that the human is a part of the natural cycle of life and death. It also incorporates a tragic recognition that he cannot totally communicate this knowledge. Set beside Vernon Watkins's interpretation of "Once it was the colour of saying" (mentioned earlier), this example of Thomas's young poetry seems neither too aesthetic nor too gentle:

> The force that through the green fuse drives the flower
> Drives my green age; that blasts the roots of trees
> Is my destroyer.
> And I am dumb to tell the crooked rose
> My youth is bent by the same wintry fever.

Here there is the beginning of the poem's self-awareness, in "I am dumb to tell," which acts temporarily as an oxymoron in this context of loud strong eloquence, ceasing to be so when read as qualified by its object, "rose."

The poem continues with a more concentrated attention to a failure of the speaker's communication with the whole natural world of which he knows himself to be part: he goes on from flowers and trees to include rocks, water, winds, the dead, and parts of his own body: "I am dumb to mouth unto my veins / How at the mountain spring the same mouth sucks," "I am dumb to tell the hanging man / How of my clay is made the hangman's lime," "I am dumb to tell a weather's wind / How time has ticked a heaven round the stars," and "I am dumb to tell the lover's tomb / How at my sheet goes the same crooked worm." The highly musical, witty, and sensuous poem declaims the natural life-death vitality, calling attention to its own language by the repetitions and permutations. It is an extreme image of utterance and of dumbness. The whole poem has the impact of oxymoron.

What is imagined, with the bizarre inventiveness of Thomas's imagination of the not-human, is a precise, rationally sustained, but extravagant image, beginning with the abstract force of the first stanza then becoming a vast invisible mouth, sucking at the mountain, created by inference from springs and their sources. Thomas is fond of images of sucking (also of breasts and milk) and they may be called infantile, and are certainly erotic, but they are presented here as part of the consistent and analytic awareness of language, and specifically the use of words and the use of tales. The word "mouth" is varied, run through the three grammatical forms, as participle, infinitive, and substantive, "mouthing," "to mouth," and "the . . . mouth." The familiar central use "I am dumb to mouth" is framed by the two unfamiliar images personifying the active flow of water and its natural (or supernatural) source. And the images are appropriate images for both sound and action, babbling and suction, which are both like and unlike human mouthings. Thomas does something with language which both Hopkins and Yeats liked to do, when he refreshes a common dead metaphor, in this case, "mouth," familiarly used in the geographical naming of rivers and seas. He defamiliarizes geographical metaphor, as he limns a magnificently grotesque image, using the synecdoche, that part which implies a whole, to image a Nature or a god creating springs and streams by strong suction, pressure, and momentum. This is inventive genius, a new sublime, yet cool enough to draw attention to its own rhetoric and act of creativity.

The image and idea of mouthing is there because the poem, like so many of Thomas's poems, is about artistic language, that feature which distinguishes the human animal, in life, from the other aspects and forms of nonhuman, and aspects of human, life. (Of course nonhuman nature does some mouthing.) The speaker complains in a form which is literal statement and a form of *occupatio*. "I am dumb": he really cannot tell the natural elements or his own body or the dead about their companionship in the death-birth cycle (made specific as the carbon and nitrogen cycles in the images of lime, clay, and tomb) but the insistent complaint makes a means of telling as it tells about not telling. It forms a passionately clamant address whose companionable caring and yearning saves the idea from being a mere matter of chemical and biological knowledge. That triple permutation and repetition isolates and to an extent abstracts the word "mouth," showing root and paradigm as in a grammar, all in one mouthing stanza, to vary and concentrate repetition. The diffusion, in all five stanzas, of the word "dumb," and of "tell" in four of them, also varies the pattern, as it makes the emphasis more simply, through sheer repetition.

There is also an ambiguity in the statement about dumbness, which can be read as saying that dumbness is an appropriate way of communicating with the nonhuman nature which can't speak our language. There is a kind of alternative truth in saying "I am dumb in order to communicate with vegetation, minerals, water, wind, earth, and the dead": this is a way of describing what will happen after death, so the poem contains the reversal of its own powerful declaration about tragic living art. I want to call it brilliantly reversible, rather than self-deconstructive.

To return to the obvious. The poem is about the natural cycle, but also about communication, in the two basic forms: telling, that is, narrating, with the suggestion also of informing; and also mouthing, that is, making words or attempts at words, but also mere voicing, sounding, making a noise—just the right word for imagining that impossible communication with wordless nature or bits of nature or forms of nature. In the last line the triple pun on "sheet" begins with "winding" sheet, moves to bedsheet, and ends with sheet of paper, with the parallel transmutation of grave worm to penis and pen, in a characteristic grim neatness, a joke that gives us just a little bit extra, in the way of meaning, wit, and resonance.

The topos of reflexivity is a figure in a poem which makes

explicit what is implicitly being said throughout the poem about creativity in the largest sense of the word. It is creativity imputed to natural causes, tracked from a growth which can make a flower explode, lively and deadly, from a stem, in a brilliant musically expressive line which speeds through fast smooth fluent monosyllables to expand in the extrasyllabic "flower." Thomas said once that "flower" was a disyllable, and it always is, pronouncedly, in the Welsh accent, though the English can drawl it as monosyllable. But even when pronounced in a non-Welsh voice the word will usually hover between monosyllable and disyllable here preserving while extending the pentameter, an end word which is a natural and beautiful product of that fuse, which is both slender green stem and lit explosive lead to fire the gunpowder or the dynamite.

The poetry is full of such powerful blendings of the explicit and implicit subject of making. In some poems the artist is clearly—deeply or shallowly—present, declaring in first line (and title), "I in my intricate image" or "In my craft and sullen art." Sometimes the artist is a dominant dramatized character in the poem, speaking as a rhetorician, a worker in language, an Aesop, a storyteller, or a poet, or some other kind of maker, a Noah, a mad person, a child playing games, a telltale, very often a Christ or a god. And there are many different forms of creativity, as well as those to be inferred from this list of makers: a dream, a fairy story, a building, a jealous imagining, a mocking, a compensatory sick fantasy.

One of his best poems about imagination is that other short but big poem, "The hunchback in the park" (CP and NP), like "After the funeral" a notebook poem disruptive of theories of maturation, since it was begun in the early thirties and published, in revised form, in 1942.

In this poem everybody is making something, in mimicry, play, and fantasy, so that the subject of creative imagination is compounded. In the earliest notebook version the creativity is confined to the hunchback, and the process of revision is an expansion of the creative theme, making everyone imaginative, and significantly including the creativity of children's play. The poet wrote down his childhood experience, and in the process of revising the poem saw more and more in that experience. This is memory as gradual comprehension, showing its powers in a growing poem. But the poet knew what the hunchback stood for right from the start: in the early version the hunchback's creation is said to be a poem, as well as an image, but this explicitness and redundancy was wisely removed in revision.

The poem was once recited in the prose context of a BBC broadcast "Reminiscences of Childhood," where it was glossed, "the bushy Red-Indian-hiding park, where the hunchback sat alone, images of perfection in his head" (QEOM, p. 6) and the park was named as Cwmdonkin as it is not in the poem. The park itself is where the narrator's memory of making begins, in his childhood play, as it was shown, more lightly, indirectly, and casually in "Patricia, Edith, and Arnold." Like the whole town, the park is also a seat of creativity, literally and metaphorically, a good and familiar site for meditation or play, public life and private relations. So the poem begins by compounding beginnings, as the park opens in the early morning, with a kind of creative fiat:

> The hunchback in the park
> A solitary mister
> Propped between trees and water
> From the opening of the garden lock
> That lets the trees and water enter.

Nature enters, and so does the hunchback, the subject of the fluent stanzaed, lightly punctuated, three-sentenced poem, felt as a perpetual and organic presence in the park:

> Like the park birds he came early
> Like the water he sat down.

And the two last stanzas reveal his occupation: like his poet his creativity blends the human with the nonhuman:

Made all day until bell time
A woman figure without fault
Straight as a young elm
Straight and tall from his crooked bones
That she might stand in the night.

The poem ends with a counterbalancing close, the image of conclusion and closure, of locking the park, "after the locks and chains" and everything else in the poem, "the railings and shrubberies / The birds the grass the trees the lakes / and the wild boys innocent as strawberries" are hustled out and loosened in a common dissolution and unmaking, an un-punctuated fluent unlocking of language, following "the hunchback / To his kennel in the dark." All the creative activity in the poem takes place in the light, framed by the dark, when the creative fiat—and that precise "fiat lux" of the vision in St. John, of which the poem is clearly aware—is undone. The poem about creativity ends with the hunchback's, and its own, uncreating, and the park's familiar warning bell tolls a long resounding echo which takes us beyond the park and its creatures to a larger sense of darkness and closure.

That creative activity is intense and generalized too. All around the hunchback's central, profound, and solitary act of making, is the imaginative companionship, the mocking boys imitating him and pretending to be sailors and tigers, in bad and good forms of creativity. The speaker recollecting his childhood sailed his boat in the fountain. The hunchback creates to enjoy perfection, making the ideal object of frustrated desire, his beloved and his opposite, out of his defect and longing. Like Philoctetes, his wound is the defect and pain compensated for by the power of the bow. As Lawrence says we all do, he sheds his sickness in the making. He creates the woman's image in order to avert the chaos of darkness, "to stand in the dark" and "the unmade park." He creates in order to leave something after he goes, "All night in the unmade park." And he creates what the maker of the poem can only infer and imagine. The little boy could only see and make fun of the hunchback, but the poet breathed a possible life and health into the remembered image. Like "Who Do You Wish Was With Us?" the poem is most fully and finely about imagining, and has its origin in imagining imagination.

Another poem in which a highly individualized creative character is imagined, "Love in the Asylum," is much less clear and plain, partly because Thomas is inventing a deranged idiolect. Though of course this is an exotic and weird language, for a character he finds congenial, like Noah the ark builder and drunken sailor, or the fetus in "If my head hurt a hair's foot," or Jesus, or God. The speaker is a patient (patients in psychiatric hospitals were then uninhibitedly called mad, even lunatic) in what was then called an asylum. Thomas was struck, like all the town, by the new asylum conspicuously built in 1931 on one of Swansea's surrounding hills; it was called Cefn Coed, and said by Thomas in one of the notebook poems "Upon your held-out hand" to leer "down the valley like a fool" (NP) That transference of madness from inmate to institution—building and furniture—is a dominant figure in this madman's speech:

> A stranger has come
> To share my room in the house not right in the head,
> A girl mad as birds
>
> Bolting the night of the door with her arm her plume.
> Strait in the mazed bed
> She deludes the heaven-proof house with entering clouds
>
> Yet she deludes with walking the nightmarish room,
> At large as the dead,
> Or rides the imagined oceans of the male wards.

She has come possessed
Who admits the delusive light through the bouncing wall,
        Possessed by the skies

She sleeps in the narrow trough yet she walks the dust
        Yet raves at her will
On the madhouse boards worn thin by my walking tears.

And taken by light in her arms at long and dear last
        I may without fail
Suffer the first vision that set fire to the stars.

Each intricate, formally set-out, but overflowing stanza is rich with Thomas's favorite devices, all of which mime a mad language. Thomas is probably the modern poet most fond of the Virgilian and Shakespearean figure of hendiadys, which here sounds aptly odd, new, simple, and yet logical, as it separates epithets, revises meanings, and distinguishes categories: "at long and dear last," a hendiadic phrase also characteristic in mutating a common expression, "at long last."

There is the transferred epithet, "the house not right in the head," a figure originating in the "notebook" poem already mentioned. Transference is continued in a sliding ambiguity, "raves. . . . / On the madhouse boards worn thin." There is the riddling simile, "mad as birds": why birds? Because if you expect them to speak our language, or think like us, they will sound and seem mad. (Virginia Woolf makes her mad Septimus in *Mrs. Dalloway* think the birds spoke Greek, recalling one of her own hallucinations.) There is the surreal visual collocation which makes good and strange sense, the Dali-like "walking tears." There is the epithet whose precise meaning slowly dawns on us, "bouncing wall." There is the allusive fantasy, "bolting the night of the door with her arm her plume," which seems to draw on at least two fairy tales.

If the love story of elective affinities seems too fantastic, it is of course a narrative idiolect. The story is told by a madman, so the feathery-armed girl with her distress and nym-phomaniac desire, riding "the imagined oceans of the male wards" may be a product, rather than an instance, of erotic delusion. And there is the marvelous conclusive revisionary *fiat*, "Suffers the first vision that set fire to the stars," which is another version of "Let there be light," but also, of course, a megalomaniac delusion of the ordinary madman who knows he is God, and of the mad arsonist making his light and starting a fire by striking a match. It is an imagination thoroughly imagined, psychologically and mythologically.

To return to "After the funeral," which I discussed in the first chapter, as an example of Thomas's adoption of a bardic role for a conspicuously Welsh subject. Thomas made this poem reflexive for an excellent reason, and in a most cunning way, incorporating a revision as part of the poem's construc-tion and control of feeling. As I said, he had written emotion-ally without retracting the emotion, and rewrote with a fine sensitive tact which let him have his grandiose sentimentality and rebuke it, especially in the lines:

(Though this for her is a monstrous image blindly
Magnified out of praise; her death was a still drop;
She would not have me sinking in the holy
Flood of her heart's fame; she would lie dumb and deep
And need no druid of her broken body).

Writing an elegy, he is coolly aware of funeral rites, but wit-tily transforms them in order to make a new compassion. In-tense feeling is combined with cool wit: "Her fist of a face died clenched on a round pain; / and sculptured Ann is sev-enty years of stone." She is allowed to engross the monumen-tal stone in a way which allows her to die and pays tribute to her endurance. And after this the poet fascinatingly hands over the responsibility of mourning to the dead woman, imagining her response and allowing her stone strength and stoicism to make the tombstone statuary. The poem works in a way which is warm and cool, personal and impersonal, passionate and aware of artifice:

These cloud-sopped, marble hands, this monumental
Argument of the hewn voice, gesture and psalm
Storm me forever over her grave . . .

When he heard that his aunt was dying of cancer, he wrote the honest, or affected or confused, letter referred to in chapter 1, about feeling no grief or sympathy for a woman who had always been loving and generous to him. The final transformation of his difficulty in mourning into poetry seems to be a remarkable example of the gap between person and work of art, which D. H. Lawrence had in mind when he advised us to trust the tale not the artist. In the compassionate praise of his poem, the poet is allowed a history, a full appearance, a release of his power, then a control and withdrawal, in what I think is the most original, ingenious and witty English elegy since Milton's "Lycidas," and which arguably does more for Ann Jones than Milton chose to do for his dead Cambridge friend, Henry King. As I have said already, in the process, Thomas also showed himself as a good critic of his own eloquence.

Another poem I have already mentioned in chapter 1, "A Refusal to Mourn the Death, by Fire, of a Child in London," is an example of an elegy which makes a space for the dead while placing the poet as a sensitively subdued figure. It is also like "The force that through the green fuse" in contemplating, questioning, and abnegating the poet's love of language. Like "The force" it insists on negatives, in the title, and in such lines as, "Never . . . shall I let pray the shadow of a sound," "I shall not murder / The mankind of her going," "Nor blaspheme . . . With any further / Elegy." The *occupatio* seems perverse, or artificial, but on pondering this difficult poem, eventually seems justified, because it recognizes the death as part of the natural cycle, and allows the poet to sublime the child with honor and dignity, insisting that the occasion is not one for elegy. Like "After the funeral," it deals, in its different way, with the moral problem of elegy, which is the appropriation by the poet of someone else's tragic occasion. He chooses to write the poem, but to insist that it is not an elegy, or is perhaps a curtailed elegy, and is a lamentation, and melancholy acceptance, of the human condition.

Some of Thomas's best lyrics, the birthday poems, deal with the poet marginally, suggesting but not centering the theme of art. "Poem in October," also mentioned in chapter 1, remembers the matrices of grown-up creativity, in parables, chapel legends, and a mother's storytelling, "the twice-told fields of infancy"; not only echoing Wordsworth and Blake but suggestively imaging the many-layered tellings of parents to children, ritualistically regenerated as parents tell their children what their parents told them, in mutuality and continuity. It is also a fine image of twice-telling memory, which repeats itself, over and over. Thomas does too, in these memory poems, in feats of variation and renewal.

The poem recalls joy becoming vocal in the boy's spontaneous and trustful whispering, uninhibited and unfrustrated and confident, not like the dumbness and mouthing in "The force that through the green fuse" or even Noah's merrily self-deprecated sawing and rumpus. The poem, like others, represents Thomas's Wordsworthian sense of the easy playful animation and animism of the child in nature. "The force that through the green fuse" represents an alienated though loving speech and communication, but these birthday poems, by remembering, dissolve the verge and cross the boundary between the human and the nonhuman phenomenal existences.

The child's recalled emotions are communicated naturally to the natural world, through the fluent run of "the trees and the stones and the fish in the tide," to get an answering music, "And the mystery / Sang alive / Still in the water and singing-birds." For the thirty-year-old man in the poem, as for Joyce's grown-up Stephen Dedalus looking back to infancy, it was storytelling time, and a very good time indeed, for parents and children. And as in some of the stories, play is inventive, mimetic, exciting, and easy. Its ease of language, though, is remade by memory's heartbreaking telling and listening, "his tears burned my cheeks and his heart moved in mine." The child is made to seem more dead than the dead as the "true/ Joy of the long dead child" is recalled as a burning song. Then the time shifts from past to future in a secular prayer for continuities, a sequence of singing, telling and remembering in which birthdays are links in the chain of natural piety. It invokes the singing of "heart's truth" as a hopeful wish for another happy return, always part of Thomas's ritual in these birthday poems. In them conventional birthday wishes are introverted, as well as being psychologically and metaphysically deepened. They are personal, but quiet in their natural-seeming self-reference, working by suggestion and implication. When poet Noah apologizes for the lofty singing image in "Prologue," he is aware of Thomas's affection for it, ceremoniously acknowledging more than one poem:

> O may my heart's truth
>   Still be sung
> On this high hill in a year's turning.

Unlike this poem, the later "Poem on his birthday" varies the stance with a third-person narrator, but the adult autobiographical references are specific. He lives in a house on stilts, is "the rhymer in the long tongued room" and a middle-aged man sharply aware of mortality. He knows his thirty-five years are "driftwood"—another image of his brotherhood in nature. The image of song is dominant, the poem "sings towards anguish," and it startlingly and originally creates a climactic credo by devising first a prayer, then a praise, a poem or poems within the poem. The poem is allowed to have its first person after all.

Thomas's inset example is first quietly introduced after a praise of a praying God, "alone / With all the living" to whom the speaker will lament, "Faithlessly":

Oh, let me midlife mourn by the shrined
    And druid herons' vows
The voyage to ruin I must run,
    Dawn ships clouted aground.

But then the song of praise, a dignified and elaborate Magnificat, and a blessing count which recalls the simple chapel hymn, "Count your blessings / Count them one by one," is introduced dramatically, with the poet's familiar first-person deprecation:

Yet, though I cry with tumbledown tongue
    Count my blessings aloud:

    Four elements and five
Senses, and man a spirit in love
    Tangling through this spun slime
To his nimbus bell cool kingdom come
    And the lost, moonshine domes,
And the sea that hides his secret selves
    Deep in its black, base bones,
Lulling of spheres in the seashell flesh,
    And this last blessing most,

    That the closer I move
To death, one man through his sundered hulks,
    The louder the sun blooms
And the tusked, ramshackling sea exults.

The last three stanzas are given up to this praise, and take the poem, like *A Portrait of the Artist as a Young Man*, from the third person to the first person, and with a very similar sense of release, commitment and affirmation, marking an emphatic and demonstrative act of creativity, a personal microlyric, a poem within the poem, which in one of the poet's most bold, precise, and triumphant assimilations of the artist to a created world, is seen to be generated and busily creating, in a world which "Spins its morning of praise." This is romantic self-consciousness at its most dazzling, ecstasy given its head, the brilliantly witty multiple meaning "spins" noting active motion, the globe's turning, and the spinning of thread and fates. But like Stephen Dedalus's villanelle, daringly introduced into Joyce's *A Portrait of the Artist as a Young Man*, as process, revision, and composition, the lyric praise is controlled, placed, carefully presented as a credo, introduced with a fiat, to be heard and seen in a dynamic process.

Another memory poem about creative childhood, and another poem all in a rush with creativity, is "Fern Hill." It begins with a fiat, in one of the poet's most complexly self-conscious signals of beginning. The ambiguous colloquial marker of beginning, a "Now," is used to assimilate the poem's present tense to its remembered past, as the past tense "I was" casts on the "Now" a shadow of its prepositional function, and the double sense emerges, two times informally and artfully and easily brought together:

Now as I was young and easy under the apple boughs
About the lilting house and happy as the grass was green,
  The night above the dingle starry,
    Time let me hail and climb
  Golden in the heydays of his eyes.

This poem also remembers a time when communication was creative and easy, as it is imagined in an inventive and articulate childish singing and playing, "I was huntsman and herdsman," and the natural world sings back, "the calves / Sang to my horn." The man-made world, merged with nature by adult idealizing and blurring memory and by childhood's animistic imagination, also responds, in "tunes from the chimneys." Time's temporary benevolence is shown as creative, and as the cause of creativity: his turning is "tuneful," and he lets the speaker have "rare morning songs." Instead of feeling his chains, the child "sang like the sea," the sea which sounds naturally and unknowingly and which is either unchained, or chained differently. But the child is being remembered, and now the poet knows that all the time he was singing in chains.

The poem's center is not simply a child's creativity. The child's imagination is revived by the creativity of his adult self. As in "The hunchback in the park," the creativity is made emphatic and clear by strong signs and symbols of beginning and ending. The child's animism and primitive (Berkleyan) idealism makes him conceive of his child's world—his conscious waking existence—as coexistent with the whole real world, even responsible for it. Like the park, it is uncreated when he sleeps and recreated when he wakes: "As I rode to sleep the owls were bearing the farm away":

> And then to awake, and the farm, like a wanderer white
> With the dew, come back, the cock on his shoulder:
>   it was all
> Shining, it was Adam and maiden.

The story isn't simply that of the child's creativity. The shining memory is placed in the creation myth by the child who has grown up to remember and re-create. It is merged, paradisiacally, with Thomas's new version of Milton's exuberant, joyful, and didactic narration of beginning, told to Adam and Eve by the angel Raphael in *Paradise Lost*.

Thomas's poems are thoroughly modernist in their self-awareness. His spellbinding confident knowledge of language warms to the complexity, strangeness, newness and bliss of creativity. But his awareness is not only an awareness of poetry, or art. In the late poem "In the White Giant's Thigh," he pays a tribute to the creative yearning of women who couldn't create in the ordinary biological way, and who, like the hunchback, converted their isolation, their loss, their pain, their defective sterility, to imagine fertility, in fantasy, wishes, and prayer—that other form of poetry Thomas liked:

> Through throats where many rivers meet, the curlews cry,
> Under the conceiving moon . . .
>
> Through throats where many rivers meet, the women pray,
> Pleading in the waded bay for the seed to flow
> Though the names on their weed grown stones are rained
>   away,
>
> And alone in the night's eternal, curving act
> They yearn with tongues of curlews for the unconceived
> And immemorial sons of the cudgelling, hacked
>
> Hill.

He imagines the lubricating water in the throat of bird, river and human being, reinventing the sympathetic magic of fertility ritual and rainmaking rites. Once more the image and ritual use song, as the "tongues of curlews" blend human and nonhuman nature. But the rites the women enact and the poet reenacts are also drama, the ancient fertility play in the phallic theater of the Cerne Abbas giant. The place and its huge image form a powerful site of imagination, and of course the chalk-hill carving is itself a work of art, made and remade by generations, "hacked" and "sawed," like Noah's ark and Thomas's poems.

"In the White Giant's Thigh" was intended to be the first section of the projected long poem, "In Country Sleep," which was not completed but exists in drafts and fragments. The incomplete but eloquent and polished fragment "In Country Heaven" uses angelic singing, and so does a holograph fair copy draft of "In Country Sleep," published in their note to that poem by Walford Davies and Ralph Maud in their edition of *The Collected Poems*. It concentrates on storytelling, not song, in the playful, very Joycean image of "All the Canterbury bells in the wild hedge / Row of the small, brown friars, / The lithe reeve and the rustling wife / Blithe in the tall telling." The allegorist in this poem, "Young Aesop fabling by the coracled Towy," was later transferred, with slight changes, to "Over Sir John's Hill," also intended as part of the sequence, and I think becoming a more interesting poem—its allegory less playful and more political—when seen in its larger context.

"Over Sir John's Hill" is an affirmative poem, where Aesop takes responsibility for an allegory which playfully casts the nonhuman creatures—hawk, sparrows, and heron—as victims and killers in a grim but also comic story of nature red in tooth and claw, and of human crime and punishment. It deliberately makes the allegory sit loosely on the natural scene in which the little birds of the bay beg the predator to attack, in which the hawk is praised and magnified, in which the heron is both a priest and a stalking killer, as well as joining in an elegiac duet with the poet. The role of Aesop also sits loosely on the narrator, singer, and recorder, who seems to be deliberately and fancifully typecast in order to make plain the amorality of the natural killings, the inappropriateness of applying the human morality play and requiem for the dead. It was intended, as I've mentioned, as part of the long poem, but when Thomas discussed the project, he made it plain that it was not intended to be affirmative, and celebratory. In some ways it is difficult to fit "Over Sir John's Hill" into the apocalyptic sequence, but if we try to imagine such company, the allegory becomes reversible, casting aspersions on the willed and conscious destructions of humanity by a comparison with the involuntary and amoral wars in nature. Thomas wrote more about this projected poem, "In Country Heaven," than he usually did, because it was an ambitious and hard concept for him, in its length and its final vision.

The enterprise was partly foreseen and unforeseen, a slow-growing, elaborate, self-generating sequence, and brings out a narrative reflexivity, interestingly relating its acts and images of telling to the psychology of memory, and to the moral and political horrors he foresaw:

> The remembered tellings, which are the components of the poem, are not all told as though they are remembered; the poem will not be a series of poems in the past tense. The memory, in all tenses, can look towards the future. (CP, p. 263)

That vision is a vastation, not a creation story. The poet draws attention to the genius of his chief narrator, "The godhead, the author, the first cause, the architect, lamp-lighter, the beginning word" (CP, p. 262), but this is a tragic reversal of Genesis and St. John, not "Let there be light" because he conceived his black epic as a destruction, a negation, and a reversal: "Let there be darkness." This divine decreation is a response to the earth's self-murder: "The Earth has killed itself. It is black, petrified, wizened, poisoned, burst" (CP, p. 262). Often in his prose, and more often in his poetry, everyday perception is reimagined, creatively perceived as creative, as the ordinary renewal and comprehension and sharing of experience, by vision and memory, by reason, the five senses and love.

His imagination of a negative creativity may suggest why he never finished "In Country Sleep." It was intended to be, at least in part, tragically open eyed in its topicality and realism, in a way which goes against the grain of Thomas's habitual praise and celebration. It is true that he intended the poem to overcome the vastation, and to tell again through the dead storytellers, in their choric utterance in the "Country Heaven," the celebrations, praises, and good news of the destroyed and remembered earth: "And the poem becomes, at last, an affirmation of the beautiful and terrible worth of the earth" (CP, p. 263). But the resurrection, through lyric and narrative, was to come about only after the black vision of destruction. The earth becomes a wasteland, which he touched on vividly and passionately, but very briefly, not in poetry but in the prose statement, a broadcast talk first published in *Quite Early One Morning,* in which he tells how the god, author, and first cause weeps and in weeping reverses the creative fiat and makes the world turns dark. The darkness is seen by the dead in Country Heaven:

> this time, spreads the heavenly hedgerow rumour, it is the Earth. The Earth has killed itself. It is black, petrified, wizened, poisoned, burst; insanity has blown it rotten; and no creatures at all. (QEOM, pp. 156–57)

Tired of accusations of philosophical pessimism, Thomas Hardy once observed drily that some temperaments become vocal in the face of tragedy. Thomas's temperament became vocal in the face of creativity, in art and nature, but he was also a political realist, and went beyond the sentimental boast that he wrote in order to praise God and man. The plans and fragments and drafts of "In Country Sleep" show that he was too intelligent not to know that the opposite was also true, that he was a celebratory poet who felt inclined to write a poetry of affirmation that imagined and incorporated, in order to overcome, a poetry of nihilism. But for him this was easier said than done.

One poem which makes an affirmation with great subtlety, also treats the subject of creativity with indirection and understatement. It is one of Thomas's plainest poems, "The Conversation of Prayer," a narrative poem in which prayers cross, the child suffering the terror and grief of bereavement, the adult blessed by the child's free joy, the child's prayer for peaceful sleep answered for the man, the man's fear of death providing a nightmare for the child. It concludes affirmatively, but the affirmation is undermined by a sense of chanciness, as Thomas writes out of a profound sense of tragic life:

> The conversation of prayers about to be said
> Turns on the quick and the dead, and the man on the stairs
> Tonight shall find no dying but alive and warm
>
> In the fire of his care his love in the high room.
> And the child not caring to whom he climbs his prayer
> Shall drown in a grief as deep as his true grave.

Prayer is a formal act of language, a communication, often patterned and musical, and this poem uses prayer to imagine an accidental or arbitrary or incomprehensible act of utterance which misses its mark, issues the message but crosses the lines wrong, but does get expressed and sent out.

In a sense the poem is about something that happens all the time in art, which crosses its wishes and answers, and may by creating an imaginary joy or grief, or by expressing its experience, console and terrify an unknown recipient. The child and the man in the poem—strangers to each other who may or may not represent different ages and stages in one life—exchange their experiences in imagination. Thomas is occupied with the articulation of feeling, its enlargement, and the response. He is using the experience to ask again Donne's famous question about the bell which tolls for everyone, some time or other. He is recording the passivity and power and oddity of communication: a friend once said, "Isn't it peculiar that Dickens should make us pity Jo [the crossing-sweeper in *Bleak House*]?"

What Dylan Thomas is certainly doing in this remarkable poem, as in some of the stories and "The force that through the green fuse," is to imagine the movement out of and away from the personal passionate need and desire, in the creation and response which so often seems involuntary, and overwhelming. He has also brilliantly hit on a lyrical narrative which admits the tragic element, but transiently avoids it.

A different version of this attempt to move beyond subjectivity is expressed in "Foster the light," a poem about imagination whose title and subject were inspired by Thomas's friend Trevor Hughes, whose experience lay behind, and came into, the story, "Who Do You Wish Was With Us?" discussed in chapters 1 and 3. This poem always interested me because in it Thomas seemed to refer to an earlier poem by Wallace Stevens, a poet very different from Thomas, though, as I mentioned in the first chapter, published with him in Roger Roughton's surrealist magazine *Contemporary Prose and Verse* in the thirties (though Stevens's poetry took a long time to make itself known in the U.K.). "Foster the light" was published in the first issue of Roughton's magazine, in May 1936. The poem apparently echoed by Thomas is "The Snow Man,"[5] with its articulation of Stevens's central aesthetic theme—the projection of the artist's imagination in a post-metaphysical world, with the concomitant sense of the limits, as well as the power, of artistic vision and knowledge. Stevens's Snow Man, with his mind of winter, stands both for the personal coloration and bias of art: he can only imagine what he sees, a world without color and animation, "the nothing that is" but also for the opposite, the scrupulous agnostic nonvisionary truth-telling of art, as he sees nothing beyond self, the "Nothing that is not there." This is Thomas's snowman too, an important figure whether he is derived from Stevens or independently created. Stevens approves his snowman, Thomas does not.

Foster the light nor veil the manshaped moon,
Nor weather winds that blow not down the bone. . . .
Master the night nor serve the snowman's brain
That shapes each bushy item of the air
Into a polestar pointed on an icicle.

The poem urges the artist to imagine beyond grief and depression, to do better than the snowman for whom, for instance, the tree—in Stevens the look and sound of pines, juniper, and spruce, in Thomas "each bushy form of the air"—can only be icily patterned and imaged. "Foster the light" uses the metaphor of the snowman, and gives him a brain, just as Stevens gave him a mind. Thomas is not setting up a snowman as model, nor articulating the ambivalence of Stevens's image of imagination, but in responding to a plea made by Hughes not to let personal emotion submerge or inhibit art, he touches on Stevens's major philosophical theme. This is art's impossible and heroic attempt to imagine but keep within the boundaries of self-experience, to project images of "unknowable reality" from the imprisoning subjectivity of life knowledge, to play the green world of nature on the blue guitar of art. The poem begins with the three words of Hughes's imperative to the artist: "Foster the light." The poet took a friend's advice.

I have only recently looked closely at the correspondence with Hughes, and the discussion by Walford Davies and Ralph Maud, who have a note on the poem and informatively quote Hughes's comment on the poem's origin:

> The poem was something of a fosterling. Trevor Hughes tells the story of its inception (in a typescript in the Special Collection Library, Buffalo):
>> In January, 1934, Dylan sent me news of his father's first illness, and some suspected illness of his own. . . . I began to type a letter. . . . I could not wait for food. (CP, p. 203)

The letter took the form of brief unfinished notes on the subject of egoism and imagination, the subject of Thomas's poem, and included the key sentences:

> How shall a man die if he has never lived, or see the beauty of the stars through the lenses of his own darkness? For so many God has never lived, the faint glimmer within them the glimmer of their own mean ego. . . . Foster the light. (CP, p. 204)

Hughes says Thomas showed him the poem six weeks later, and suggests that the poet's "dissatisfaction" with it (of which the only evidence seems to be extensive revision and the word "clumsy" in a comment to Pamela Hansford Johnson) derives from its external origin, its not being "a direct and ecstatic inspiration" (CP, p. 204). The editors find this dissatisfaction confirmed in Thomas's words to Desmond Hawkins, urging its publication: "Do for sweet Christ's sake use the one beginning Foster the light, nor veil the cunt-shaped moon" (CL, p. 203). This ribald irreverence need not mean anything beyond panic about replacing a poem already printed and the inability to resist facetious self-deprecation and rude jokes. The editors find a possible trace of Hughes's influence in the appearance of "God in the last stanza" but conclude that the poem "urges myriad and cosmic activities, more things, we feel, than were dreamt of in Hughes' philosophy" (CP, p. 204).

I think this is hard on Hughes. The poem is a direct response to Hughes's notes about not being blinded by ego, and the response is an important one. The poem was extensively revised, and some of the most telling images, including that of the snowman's imagination, took some time to evolve (NP, pp. 214, 229). The poem articulates the imagination's grasp of opposition and difference, bringing out Thomas's love of dialectic and antithesis, and implicitly celebrating Thomas's refusal to anthropomorphize nature, though its last stanza returns to the familiar subject of life's engrossment with death, "Who gave these seas their colour in a shape / Shaped my clayfellow." None of this is precisely what Hughes is talking about, but I think it comes close to it.

The common subject, of Thomas's poem and Hughes's notes, is imagination's push toward depersonalizing emotion, moving beyond the momentary self. It is part of an ongoing discussion, important to both men. Thomas's letters to Hughes, as I said in chapter 3, tried to persuade him out of morbidity into the creativity Thomas believed he was capable of, and on this occasion Hughes is telling Thomas, afflicted by anxiety and grief for his father and himself, to do likewise. Hughes also provided his friend with a rich image, and a title, for imaginative effort, in that imperative, sensitive, and ambiguous "Foster." Some years later Thomas was to write one of his best stories—I think his very best story—under the influence of his friendship with Hughes, and the poem, like the story, is also about imagination's attempt to impersonalize itself. This is something not experienced for long by Raymond Price, the Hughes character, though achieved, as the story proves, by its narrator, the Dylan character. "Foster the light" is the poetic twin, and perhaps the progenitor, of "Who Do You Wish Was With Us?" In it Thomas engages, however briefly, knowingly or unknowingly, and for the only time, with Stevens's daring, sophisticated, modern, postmetaphysical refusal to anthropomorphize. (Stevens entertained the concepts of an animated and knowable universe through the "necessary angel" of imagination.) Thomas briefly mentions Stevens in his letters, but it took Trevor Hughes to start the connection, and inspire one of Thomas's most important reflexive poems.

5. The Green Poet

The Theme of Nature

There are very few of Thomas's poems which do not offer a meditation on nature. Many can be called poems about nature. As I have been showing, some consider art and nature, with equal or unequal emphasis. More rarely, some are about love and nature.

In "The force that through the green fuse" and "Fern Hill," Thomas is meditating on art and nature at one and the same time. Neither subject is subordinate, and both are imaginatively ingrained in the language, music, and form. The poems are Janus-faced, looking evenly in two directions. They are flexible forms, like those outlines shaped one way like a face, the other like a vase. They are poems which almost succeed in crossing the threshold from human nature to nonhuman nature, which attempt to assert—and demonstrate—that such a threshold does not exist. But each good poem is an individual entity, and each poem makes its imaginative statement—perhaps "essay" is a better word—in a different way.

These two big poems are both occupied with greenness, in its many meanings. I believe that Thomas is a green poet, who fully understands the politics of greenness, anticipating our present wishes and efforts to care for the globe, our polluted environment, and to displace the human animal from a still prevailing arrogant centrality.

Thomas fills his poetry with greenness, and admired earlier poets, like Traherne and Blake, who shared his celebratory and re-creative sense of sensuous and symbolic significances of green. In his twinned "Nurse's Songs," one bitter, sterile and jealous, the other liberated, fresh and enabling, Blake provides a model for comprehending and expressing the sense of greenness. Thomas follows this model, explicitly or implicitly, in "The force that through the green fuse" and he wrote "I am in the path of Blake" (CL, p. 79, quoted in CP, p. 183.) But long before his English models, the medieval Welsh poets, Dafydd ap Gwilym and his contemporary and friend Gruffydd ap Adda, colored their nature and love lyrics with many shades of green, and Iolo Morgannwg, four centuries later, wrote "The Poet's Arbour in the Birch-wood," almost as green as "Fern Hill" or "The force that through the green fuse."

"The force that through the green fuse" names the natural force as green, then in a leap of metaphor both new and traditional, immediately includes the human life, "my green age," in which the old use of green, as in the "green judgment" of Cleopatra's salad days and the common sense of "silly-ignorant-innocent," is transmuted by association with the plant's stem, and becomes a welcome hybrid, meaning young and fresh. "Drives my green age": the poem proves, or demonstrates, in the way poems do prove, or demonstrate, what it says. It does so by a forceful impassioned repetition of the word, and by the cunning intrication of a set of associations which initiate or make a language change. Green is made new, and since it is itself the sign and symptom of nature made new, there is a special wit, liveliness, and freshness about its renewals. Green is, of course, in politics as in poetry, wrenched from literal meanings for the purposes of metaphor, belonging as it does, chiefly though not exclusively, to the least regarded, vegetable, part of creation. There are green birds and insects and reptiles, but one of the puzzles of science is the absence of green mammals, the so-called green monkey not being an exception. So the human adoption of the color for the raised ecological consciousness is both especially ironic and especially appropriate. This choice of a nonhuman color to symbolize ecological justice offers a semantic apology for anthropocentrism.

The epithet "green," shared by human and nonhuman nature, here makes a statement about the identity, or intimacy, of both, and starts off the sequence of statements about a natural unity—what Coleridge called the unity of being—which does not depend at all on greenness, as the poet turns to rocks, water, wind, clay, lime, sheets, and bodies. (As in recent political usage, Thomas's green is both taken literally and knowingly deployed as metaphor for nature.) As I have said, he imagines nature as a force, but the word "force" is too conceptual, so it is animated but not anthropomorphized, magnified, and bodied, with organs: "The mouthing streams" and "the hand that whirls the water in the pool." Sensation and abstraction are made to cross and kiss, (to double-cross, in Thomas's own pun) and to conceive a new creature, as Joyce creates a physical but also mythological Finnegan in the fluidity and fragmentariness of his last novel's process, a form of necessary chaos out of which to bring order. Thomas's short poem isn't as chaotic, but it is dynamic, fast, teeming, rushing and swirling in movement, and filled with images of rushing, swirling, streaming, pressing, and propulsion, explosion, sap rise, growth, water flow, wind, erection, tumescence, chemical cycle—and also breakdown, execution, decay, dissolution, detumescence.

"Fern Hill" is about his green age, and is both like and unlike "The force that through the green fuse" in its playful and serious insistence on greenness. Its many greens compose the greenness of the first world, in the lyric which is Thomas's "Paradise Lost" and "Paradise Regained." It tells, like Milton's first epic, and as a narrative inset, the story of creation. I have already emphasized Thomas's imagery of art—the play, the games, the dreams, the songs, the stories—and these, like the green age in the sonnet, are colored by the green of the natural world in which they are located, with which they play, and which they praise.

It is a Rhapsody in Green, repeating and permuting the green images. Its green goes back to the "Green as beginning" in the final poem of the earlier sonnet sequence "Altarwise by owl-light." Greenness begins in the title, Fern Hill, a place-name title which remembers but slightly though significantly changes the name of his first green place, rechristening his aunt's farm, Fernhill, as Fern Hill, formalizing, analyzing, carefully enunciating, separating its syllables and words, emphasizing the two natural elements of vegetation and earth, making a title, referring to a hill as well as a man-made farm, appropriately renaming the experience he is recalling and resurrecting.

There is green in each of its six, flowing, occasionally rhyming, highly assonant and alliterative stanzas. (This was first pointed out, as far as I know, by Henry Treece, though he does little beyond making the observation.) The repeated greens are linked and varied, emerging as themes but also working like notes and chords in music, and shifted from literal to metaphorical meanings, as images in poetry.

In the first stanza the speaker was "happy as the grass was green" in his young days, naturally, freshly, and brightly happy, now using a new comparison for which there are familiar analogues, especially "happy as the day was long." There is a conversion to greenness. The second stanza is the only one in which "green" appears twice, as if to reinforce the beginning and show the key image, but in both appearances the color becomes metaphorical: "as I was green and carefree" and "And green and golden I was huntsman and herdsman"; the first perhaps a touch more abstract, the second made more sensuous by that companionable "golden" and the suggestion of the huntsman and herdsman in green fields and woods. In the third stanza the word returns to color, but startlingly, "fire green as grass" reminding us that fire can burn green but at the same time turning up an unexpected variation, in a comparison which begins by sounding traditional, like the two earlier "greens," and of course contains a traditional comparison, but ends by amazing sense and mind. In the fourth stanza we have what is perhaps the strangest of all these greens, when the first horses are imagined "walking warm / Out of the whinnying green stable." And in the fifth and last stanza we go back to the early tradition-hallowed metaphors of green meaning young and silly and ignorant and innocent, but here defamiliarized by its new collocation, "green and dying." This suggests both the early beginning of dying and the youthfulness and silliness and ignorance and innocence of all ages.

Green is dominant, but it is not the only color, though we get a favored palette rather than a complete spectrum. Green is qualified by the slightly less frequently used "golden," which is like green both a color word and an old traditional metaphor. It appears once in the first stanza, twice in the second, and once in the fifth, but twice in a prominent position at the beginning of lines with parallel syntax, "Golden in the heydays of his eyes" and "Golden in the mercy of his means." We have only one "white," a wanderer white and the dew," one dark, "flashing into the dark," and one vivid metaphorical, new and old, blue, "at my sky blue trades." Here the blue associates the boy's "horn" with Little Boy Blue, coincides with Wallace Stevens's emblematic color for art (as in "The Blue Guitar" which must play the green world), and in a brilliant intuition chooses the perfect color for the innocent joys of childhood. Like the two greens in "The force that through the green fuse," the colors identify and join the human and nonhuman natural world, all its creatures and elements made new and strange.

Art and nature are inextricably fused in the poet's new creation story, which remakes Milton and uses the child's wild and brave imagination to present the bizarre image of those horses "walking warm." It brings together the extremes of creativity, the great English poet's epic, and the child's-play dream: both are creative, and also re-creative, as they remake the Bible story. It also brings together the extremes of unprofessional creativity, in memory and dream. And of course the modern poet binds the epic, the play, the dream, and the memory together, in a lyric which rings with the joy of knowing nature and art.

The horses are warm, because they are newborn, just out of the wet womb, because they are walking into the heat of the first light, and because horses always feel warm to human touch. They are walking out of a green stable not just because they are a child's horses, or because a poet can make a stable green, as Stephen Dedalus made a rose green, but also because, though stables aren't green, this one is brand-new. It is the very first stable for the very first horses and the poet gives it an appropriately original color. Thomas, like the Green politicians and parties, uses the color sign of that least privileged part of nature, vegetation, which all of us, even vegetarians, destroy. And he uses it in a way which brings out the reason and the strangeness of its signature. Violently yet quietly unsettling man's centrality, "green" is made to stand for the basic fundamental creative principle or life force.

"On to the fields of praise"—where else, in a poem about wondering at wonderful creation, and restoring the innocent excited playful eye, touch, and imagination of childhood most properly, in order to wonder? Thomas gave a broadcast on the "Poems of Wonder" (TB, pp. 63–73), and though he didn't mention the color green, most of the poets he read in that talk imagine greenness—Vaughan, Marvell, Traherne, Blake, de la Mare, and John Crowe Ransom. Like them, and also like Milton and Lawrence, both powerful influences on his work, Thomas himself wrote a poetry which peels habit from vision to make the stale and tired reader wake up to wonder. A century and a half apart, the romantic Coleridge[1] and the Russian formalist Victor Shklovsky in various discussions of *ostranenie*[2] insist that art makes things strange. There can be few better twentieth-century proofs of art's creative defamiliarizing than this poem.

In a now familiar letter to Pamela Hansford Johnson, who like Vernon Watkins, but earlier, stimulated Thomas by ideas and poetry, he criticized her for attempting to write poems about the unity of being without showing the relationship of parts of nonhuman nature not only to the human creature, but to each other. As soon as he formulates his ideal you see that it is a hard thing to write because it is a hard thing to imagine:

> Though you talk all through of the relationship of yourself to other things, there is no relationship at all between the things you example. If you are one with the swallow and one with the rose, then the rose is one with the swallow. Link together these things you speak of; show, in your words & images, how *your* flesh covers the tree & the tree's flesh covers you. (CL, p. 79)

So how does Dylan Thomas do what he advises, link and show the link? The linking and the showing are matters of imagination, not willed craft, and his imaginative linkings are various. One way is through transformative imagery, as in the new hybrid epithet "green," half-literal color and half-metaphorical quality, and the old hybrids of the parsed permuted "mouth" which are first shown to cover human and vegetable life, then human and mineral life. Another way is through the embodiment and individuation of a placed and imagined passionate vision, the madman's, the god's, or the child's, which merges and mingles parts in a new-made whole, like the animated asylum, or the freshly imaged stable matrix.

These are complex and elaborate transformations and characterizations, extending over lengths of language, but Thomas is also very good at jamming together and uniting differences and disparates briefly, in a compound word. One example, from "Poem on his Birthday," is "mustardseed sun," a brilliantly plural joining through unlikenesses: one object is vegetable and one a star, one very small and one very large, one graspable and everyday, one remote and not wholly known, one a culinary aid, the other essential to life; and through the likenesses: both are natural objects, both are dense bright yellow, both round, and both provide intense heat. The result is the kind of thing which happens in the ancient Japanese form of haiku, which may in small compass collate two experiences, neither of which is made a subordinate or vehicle for the other. This is a compressed way of showing the things in the nonhuman world related to each other, and such images are characteristic original imprints of juxtaposition or comparison which relate without the hierarchy implicit in the making of metaphor. It is a form of rhetoric perfected for a decentering of the human vision.

There are other powerful examples in this magnificent poem: for instance, the "sandgrain day," "thunderclap spring," "ramshackle sea," and the "thistledown fall." These are all images like the mustardseed sun which bring together natural objects from different categories, forming compounds which refuse to subordinate either element, and refuse or resist separation into the conventional rhetorical components of tenor (subject signified) and vehicle (carrier or signifier of subject). The day is like the sand grain in being small, one amongst many, uncountable, light and bright, but the conjunction tells us as much about the sand grain as the day. The thunderclap coexists with the spring, rather than simply illustrating its explosive bursts of arrival. Thistledown does almost as much for the fall, of which it is a part, as the fall does for the thistledown, the phrase rejecting the instrumental element at work in most synecdoche as in metaphor and simile. The sea makes the shackled ram more rough, turbulent, dangerous, violent, and wild, drawing them both closer to the human being in his shore lookout. But the bucking ram makes the tusk-curved waves and tides more uninhibited, sexual, dangerous and intransigent as they obey the necessities of their regulation and rhythm. This metaphor also takes us back, like so many of Hopkins's images, to etymology, to discover that the dictionary does not give what I assumed to be the origin of the word and image, but merely guesses—with an O.E.D. "perhaps"—at possible derivations, none of which seem as plausible as the one suggested by Thomas's component-conscious compound. Thomas invents—or perhaps reinvents and discovers—the etymology, by placing an existing compound in an inventive context which makes it strange and makes us analytic. This poem's image set (noticeably but not uniquely) brings together parts of nature as equalities, so that the two syllables of ramshackle, whatever its origin, are joined and re-created as a hobbled strong sexual creature.

As I have said, these compounds work like haiku. The sea is compared with a shackled animal, the day with a grain of sand, the spring with a thunderclap, the fall with thistledown, and we accept and admire the aptness, which does the work of a precise detailed substantiation, which is not Thomas's way with nature. But there is companionship not subordination, demonstrating—or rather dramatizing—that relationship between aspects of the natural world which Thomas explained to Pamela Hansford Johnson. There is reciprocity, as in haiku. Though several Thomas critics convincingly interpret Thomas's vision of natural unity as religious, sometimes pantheistic, sometimes Christian, it may also be read as an agnostic poetry, a physical rather than a metaphysical vision, an acceptance of the human being's place in what Wordsworth called the very world in which we live, without invoking the supernatural—which after all involves hierarchy and hegemony—except as metaphor, "fabulous, dear God," who seems to be invoked as Wallace Stevens—great postmetaphysical poet of the green world—recognized the necessary angel of our human imagination.

Thomas also joins the poetry of nature with love poetry, which he writes more rarely than most poets. One of his best love poems is the extraordinary "Into her lying down head," which he describes as a "poem about modern love" (CL, p. 455). It is like some of the other poems I have mentioned—"Where once the waters of your face," for instance—in presenting an ambiguous balance and relationship of tenor and vehicle, so that at first it is possible to read it—perhaps impossible not to read it—as offering two faces: is it a love poem in which the natural world is a metaphor, or a poem about nature in which human love is a metaphor? If we conclude, as I did after many readings, that the first is the most plausible reading, this is backed by Thomas's exegesis, offered to Vernon Watkins in the letter I have just quoted.

It turns out to be a poem about jealousy, but the extensive metaphors of mineral and bird make it also a proving and a linking, another poem about the unity of being. The display of unity is moving in itself but also makes the human pair, and their needs, desires and severance, larger, more intense, and more powerful. This is seen most clearly in the last section, where Thomas's favored images of sand and bird come together, linked with each other as well as linked with the human loving—and hating:

> Two sand grains together in bed,
> Head to heaven-circling head,
> Singly lie with the whole wide shore,
> The covering sea their nightfall with no names;
> And out of every domed and soil-based shell
> One voice in chains declaims
> The female, deadly, and male
> Libidinous betrayal,
> Golden dissolving under the water veil.

Sand and water here form a remarkable image both of married love and promiscuity, and though they may eventually be seen as metaphors of a human situation, so neatly apt but weirdly unlike, so particularized is the image of coupled sand grains, close and compact as sleeping or coupled lovers, the wide expanse of beach, and the appearance of soft yellow sand in water, that the images offer a statement in themselves, suggestive of sexual love but also of a companionable proximity of mineral items. The natural world appears to create a sense of huge collective extension, and amorphous fluidity, shape taking and shape losing. The shell also takes its place in this drama, the dome suggesting amplitude and space, the "soil-based" position a tethering. Sand and sea and shell story are followed by an equivalent bird version, with similar suggestions of texture and companionably fitting bodies but with its own impression of joy: the sand grains were content, perfectly fitted, but the bird is ecstatic, welcoming both bliss and destruction, which the speechless sand grains merely suffer:

> A she bird sleeping brittle by
> Her lover's wings that fold tomorrow's flight,
>> Within the nested treefork
>> Sings to the treading hawk
> Carrion, paradise, chirrup my bright yolk.

The last movement doubles images of grass and stone, not suggesting a pairing but with a scrupulous accuracy, solitude and anonymity for the stone, but company and membership for the grass blade:

> A blade of grass longs with the meadow,
> A stone lies lost and locked in the lark-high hill.

We finally return to the human creatures, in a total and profound presentation of two points of view, the amoral view of nature, and the human sexual and social suffering which can't reach that larger natural view as it suffers. Humanity is presented in a series of compressed images which are sensuous but need intellectual unpacking: nakedness, implying companionship with the unclothed, so unprotected and undecorated air; innocence but only "between wars"; lust, secret, and uninhibited in the cause of life-force fertility, but also the private and social dimension of jealousy, solitude, and enmity. But we return to the larger viewpoint as the "severers," the deaths, obliterate the personal moralities and passions. The last image of faithless sleep makes another scrupulously accurate observation:

> Open as to the air to the naked shadow
>> O she lies alone and still,
>> Innocent between two wars,
> With the incestuous secret brother in the seconds to
>> perpetuate the stars,
>> A man torn up mourns in the sole night.
> And the second comers, the severers, the enemies from
>> the deep
> Forgotten dark, rest their pulse and bury their dead in
>> their faithless sleep.

In such a reticently and obscurely narrated love story, rendering the emotions of desire and jealousy and anger, the natural world stands out in a vivid particularity. (It is a little like the way in which an organ or object, displaced in cubist painting, may stand out in relief and new close-up.) But what is impressive about that particularity is its convincing characterization of the sand, water, bird, grass, stone and hill as live, individual, active participants. For instance, as I've said, the grass blade is allowed to long—to have a form or purpose and a belonging—while the stone is locked, imprisoned but also companioned. Sometimes the recognition of a natural object is registered simply through a precise image: for instance, "brittle" is just right for the light-boned bird, and the nonhuman amorality of the slung together "carrion, paradise," perfectly apt. The nonhuman phenomena can only be described, as scrupulously as possible, by the human creature standing on the threshold of their existence, doing his best to invent a language for his empathy, allowing them to refuse to be subordinates, instruments, and symbols.

Nature is wonderingly and wonderfully imagined, as nature, and even when human emotional and ethical language is used, as in "libidinous," "love," "longs," and "lost," it is not farfetched or inappropriate. The nonhuman identities and relations are never romanticized in this poem which is both a highly original, strange, love lyric and one of Thomas's best nature poems.

It is a poem which has always reminded me of one of Lawrence's best, but not especially typical, love poems, "The Ballad of a Second Ophelia," whose bright yolk and interdevastation of human, animal, fruit and blossom Thomas's piece echoes, so I was delighted to find Thomas quoting three stanzas of Lawrence's poem as one he admired (CL, p. 558). (He had already written this poem, but wasn't reading Lawrence for the first time.) Its ejaculatory and ecstatic eroticism is also like the tone and feeling of Lawrence's poem. "Chirrup my bright yolk" compounds celebration of the egg, distress for its spilling, and the endearment of a bird's little language, and like the language composed for the unborn child in "If my head hurt a hair's foot," this scrap of idiolect is piercingly live and vibrant, another new language, freshly minted for a mother bird, though like Lawrence's "Cluck, my yellow darlings!"—included in Thomas's quotation—using traditional little-language bird words too.

Like many seaside children, Thomas passed time lounging and watching, as well as playing and exploring, on the sands. He knows the soft, fine, gritty feel of it: his sand imagery is textural—in "From Love's First Fever" the sand spits—as well as visually evocative of the varied flat sand and dunes of the Gower peninsula. He knows the sound of sand too, and in the meditative and joyous "We lying by seasand," there is no particular seascape invoked, but we are brought close to what they all have in common, sand and sea.

> The heavenly music over the sand
> Sounds with the grains as they hurry
> Hiding the golden mountains and mansions
> Of the grave, gay, seaside land.

This seems like a composite seascape, dune country recalled in those golden mountains, the gay seaside land, the populated Swansea beach or South Gower beaches, the more isolated feel of rock and tide watch in the remoter Rhossilli or North Gower country. The scurry of sand is there too.

But the poem's sensuous nature imagery is a vehicle for feeling. The poem utters an unusually simple cry, in a laconic clipped language which Thomas probably learned from Auden, whom he disparages at times but admired:

> We lying by seasand, watching yellow
> And the grave sea . . .
>
> Watch yellow, wish for wind to blow away
> The strata of the shore and down red rock;
> But wishes breed not, neither
> Can we fend off rock arrival,
> Lie watching yellow until the golden weather
> Breaks, oh my heart's blood, like a heart and hill.

He uses the silence and stillness and beauty of the scene as a sounding board for the heart's longing. "Yellow" resonates like green in other poems, and like green is wonderfully substantiated, in the substantive of the two key watching lines. It has its own assonant mellow melody, like a hollow shell, like Billie Holiday singing "Sweet and Mellow." That short move from the metaphorical heart's-blood to the simile "like a heart" is simple but daring, breaking and starting up within short compass in a way expressive of the heartbreak it describes but doesn't quite name. The final collocation of heart and hill manages to feel for the broken hill as well as the broken heart, establishing both as strong but vulnerable objects of care.

Though less strikingly than "Into her lying down head," this is another one of many examples of the poet's love poetry for nature. This is often written—and imagined—without the detailed particularizations of nature poets like Dorothy Wordsworth or Hopkins. Blake pulls off the same trick of convincingly embracing objects in an abstract, rather than an individualized, apostrophe. His blade of grass, his grains of sand, his robin redbreast, and his pebble are very like similar natural objects in Thomas's animations.

Some of Thomas's early poems are written, as Yeats said of his own much more romantically desirous, but less erotic, early love poems, in desire and longing. But here too the imagining of the natural world often powerfully displaces the human center, and pushes itself sturdily and individually forward. This is what happens in "A grief ago," where the desolations and pleasures of love are done in substantial nature imagery. In "She who was who I hold, the fats and flower," for instance, the bodily "fats" and the metaphorical flower, linked as so often by a pun—the cooking pun—make a strong image, new and traditional, for woman's flesh and beauty, while "a chrysalis unwrinkling in the iron" is a literal example of birth and an adroit, unusually subtle, phallic symbol.

"From Love's First Fever" is another green poem (with some yellow) which particularizes the growth of a human creature through natural images:

Shone in my ears the light of sound,
Called in my eyes the sound of light.

And yellow was the multiplying sand,
Each golden grain spat life into its fellow,
Green was the singing house.

The poem's images are particular and complex, and sometimes synaesthetic, joining the mineral and animal in that
wonderful spitting image, which is sandily dry, wet, and
stinging. In that personal and radical revision of Yeats's singing school, the green singing house, there is a fusion of what
is literally animal and vegetable and metaphorically human.
As the sand grains spit life into each other, as I've mentioned,
they sting sharply and grittily like actual sand, and they are
also given an imaginary method of reproduction animistic
but also physically apt, thoroughly felt.

Once more the metaphorical vehicle for the human story
and situation is unsubdued, and here it is not only strongly
particularized by being realized through sensations of look
and feel, but is itself complicated by being imagined in ani-
mating human terms—"spat life into its fellow"—so that
the vehicle in its turn becomes tenor. Like the ambiguous
narrative of "Where once the waters of your face," this cel-
lular compounding of metaphor makes a love poem a nature
poem too.

Something similar happens in "A Refusal to Mourn the
Death, by Fire, of a Child in London," which I described in
the last chapter as holding together the subjects of art and
death. It also presents itself as a nature poem, and contains a
powerful rejection of anthropocentricity:

Never until the mankind making
Bird beast and flower
Fathering and all humbling darkness
Tells with silence the last light breaking
And the still hour
Is come of the sea tumbling in harness
And I must enter again the round

Zion of the water bead
And the synagogue of the ear of corn.

This poem whose apocalyptic metaphors blend Christian and Jewish temples in easy companionship begins by equalizing mankind and the rest of nature, in that wonderfully dignified beginning vision—in which there shall be no more sea, as well as no more land—where those principles of power, "making" and humbling, stand strongly together, to act out the stated unity of being. This is a part of the poem's curious action of *occupatio*, through which the speaker refuses to mourn for what is a tragic wasted young life and death because he is unwilling to separate death from life, and insists on celebrating the natural circulation and recycling of nature. (How could anyone with this kind of accepting and enabling imagination sympathize with nationalism?) It would be a mistake to think his position was apolitical. As I have said, Thomas was a good untheoretical caring grassroots Socialist, who said on at least one occasion that the poet had a global responsibility, and should be in touch with what was happening on this planet.

Thomas's imagination leaps to generalize, and abstract, the human condition. Sometimes he does so while sympathizing with the individual—and poetically individualized—creature, like the hunchback, Ann Jones, and Raymond's dying brother; sometimes, most extraordinarily, without individualizing human features and feelings at all, as in the speech of the unsexed fetus, or in the feeling for sap driven through stem, or in this elegy for a dead child and all the dead, human, vegetable, and mineral. (Thomas, like Blake, has a soft spot for stones.)

Without creating hard-and-fast categories and compartments, I think it important to distinguish between the handful of character poems, which are always lyrical, but are also narrative poems, and more "purely" and concentratedly lyrical poems like "The force that through the green fuse," and "A Refusal to Mourn," which avoid, fragment, or reduce narrative and character, to dwell intensely on sensation and feeling.

These highly emotional poems present the human element by generalization and abstraction, but because they are lyrically impassioned, what is made general and abstract is also made fresh, lively, and particular. In "The force that through the green fuse" and "A Refusal to Mourn," the human element is generalized and abstracted because Thomas is taking, in a tremendous imaginative essay, the vertiginous viewpoint and remarkably long perspective from which human nature is grasped as part of nature. He manages to assimilate the human element, as he believes the life force assimilates it, to rocks and stones and trees, or to substitute some of his favorite nonhuman images for those of the less green, and more hesitant, conservative, romantic, and compromised pantheist Wordsworth, to ferns, foxes, stems, sand grains, air, water, herons and hawks. The human being, especially the poet using his language as personally and passionately and particularly as poets can, cannot exactly comprehend or imagine the nonhuman phenomenal world which he contemplates, but this is what Thomas seems to achieve. It is perhaps that touch of genius which makes his very early poems so brilliant, depending as they do not on what is learned but on what is imagined in sensuous and emotional contact—the germinal experience. It seems odd that someone who was so nurtured and extroverted to participate in social culture could create or inhabit this interiority of kinship with the green world.

Two final comments. Dylan Thomas's articulated sense of natural unity makes any suggestion of provincial self-consciousness seem irrelevant, certainly for the understanding and appreciation of his poems and stories. More importantly, it explains why he could go on mining these adolescent poems for so long, revising their language, often expanding their action and scene, but keeping the germinal experience, intuitive and imaginative. Thomas is sometimes judgmentally described as immature or infantile, but I'd like to turn this analysis round and propose that he is Wordsworth's best philosopher, that lost visionary child who felt itself in easy relationship with the rest of creation, that past creative self the mature Wordsworth labored unceasingly to recall and restore. Like Wordsworth, but without the sense of loss through growth, Thomas articulated a preserved sense of the childhood intimacy with the natural world, the freedom and excitement of playing in nature, the vision of, the fusion with, "the splendor in the grass, the glory in the flower."

In much of his splendid poetry he found a language, rooted in the adolescent writing, for presenting that sense of unity, a unity of the observer with what is observed. When he writes the poem which begins "I, in my intricate image, stride on two levels," he is speaking Cartesianly about the ghost-laying poet, "the brassy orator" containing the ghost who holds "hard in death's corridor," but he also discovers a language for natural unity, a poetry like that of the great classical haiku poets, Bashō and Buson, who imagine images, narratives, and patterns without metaphorical subordinations, for expressing union and equality.

Thomas's intricate image in which he strides on two levels is an original vision of the human animal as language maker, companioned by the nonhuman animal, vegetable, and mineral phenomena, which only the human language maker is empowered to identify and to articulate, easily, frustratedly, joyfully, and bitterly. The politics and the aesthetics of this poetry are profound, and its art rare.

Notes

1: THE REGIONAL POET

1. Seamus Heaney, "The Regional Forecast," in *The Literature of Region and Nation*, ed. R. P. Draper (Basingstoke: Macmillan, 1989).

2. Stephen Spender, "A Romantic in Revolt," review of *Dylan Thomas: Collected Poems, 1934–1952, The Spectator*, 5 December 1952. This brilliant review is too often quoted only for the brief speculation about Welsh bardic influence. On rereading it I was struck by Spender's praise of Thomas's "high intelligence," his perception that the poetry keeps intellect in its place, and his recognition of the Welsh poet's regional stroppiness, to be put beside Heaney's opinion (quoted on p. 5) of Thomas's deferential provincialism. Spender perceives, "He is also the tough boy from Wales with 'the gift of the gab' and a suspicion of London and all it stands for: a kind of literary Lloyd George, breaking up an Asquithian conspiracy of Oxford and Cambridge who ruled the roost when he came to town."

3. Aneurin Talfan Davies, "William Barnes, Gerard Manley Hopkins, Dylan Thomas: The Influence of Welsh Prosody on Modern English Poetry," in *Proceedings of the Third Congress of the International Comparative Literature Association* (The Hague: Mouton, 1962); and *Dylan: Druid of the Broken Body* (Swansea: Christopher Davies, 1977).

4. Katharine Loesch, *Welsh Poetic Syntax and the Poetry of Dylan Thomas* (Denbigh: Transactions of the Honorable Society of Cymmrodorion, 1979).

5. Alan Llwyd, "*Cynghanedd* and English Poetry," *Poetry Wales* 14 (summer 1978). This special issue of the journal valuably deals with Welsh traditional forms.

6. Ibid.

7. Barbara Hardy, *The Advantage of Lyric* (London: Athlone, 1977).

2: THE MODERNIST POET

1. T. S. Eliot, "Ulysses, Order and Myth," *The Dial*, November 1923.

2. Loesch, *Welsh Poetic Syntax*, p. 48.

3. George Thomas, "Dylan Thomas and Some Early Readers," *Poetry Wales* 9 (autumn 1973).

4. Loesch, *Welsh Poetic Syntax*.

5. *Contemporary Poetry and Prose*, May 1936, July 1936.

3: DRAMATIC, NARRATIVE, LYRIC

1. Louis Berrone, "Two James Joyce Essays Unveiled: 'The Centenary of Charles Dickens' and 'L'Influenza Letteraria Universale del Rinascimento,'" *Journal of Modern Literature* 1 (February 1976).

4: THE REFLEXIVE POET

1. Samuel Taylor Coleridge, *Biographia Literaria*.

2. Linden Peach, *The Prose Writing of Dylan Thomas* (Totowa, N.J.: Barnes and Noble Books, 1988).

3. *A Prospect of the Sea*, ed. Daniel Jones (London: J. M. Dent, 1968).

4. Vernon Watkins, introduction to *Dylan Thomas: Letters to Vernon Watkins* (London: J. M. Dent and Faber, 1957).

5. Wallace Stevens, "The Snow Man," in *Harmonium* (New York: Knopf, 1923).

5: THE GREEN POET

1. Coleridge, *Biographia Literaria*, chap. 13.

2. See, for instance, Victor Shklovsky, "Art as Technique" (1917), reprinted in *Russian Formalist Criticism: Four Essays,* trans. and ed. Lee T. Lemon and Marion J. Reis (Lincoln: University of Nebraska Press, 1965).

Index

Ackerman, John, 17, 18, 62–63

Ambler, Eric, 41

Arnold, Matthew, 6

Ash, John, 42

Ashbery, John, 42

Auden, W. H., 6, 15, 106, 145

Austen, Jane, 32

Babel, Isaac, 26

Barnes, William, 11, 34

Bashō, 150

Beethoven, Ludwig von, 40

Blake, William, 118, 132–33, 137, 146

Botticelli, Sandro, 49

Breton, André, 43

Brontë, Charlotte, 90

Burns, Robert, 49

Buson, 150

Byron, Lord George Gordon, 36

Carroll, Lewis, 41

Cefn Coed (Swansea), 21, 114

Chagall, Marc, 49, 56

Chaucer, Geoffrey, 87

Chekhov, Anton, 66

Chomsky, Noam, 83

Coleridge, Samuel Taylor, xiii, 26, 51–52, 68, 87, 105, 134, 138

Contemporary Poetry and Prose, 26–27

Craigynos, 68

Cummings, E. E., 26

Cwmdonkin Park (Swansea), 19–20, 21, 22, 25, 46–47, 94, 112–13

cynghanedd, 11–12, 34

Daffydd ap Gwilym, 10, 13, 133

Dali, Salvador, 115

Davies, Aneurin Talfan, 9–10

Davies, W. H., 85

Davies, Walford, 28, 56, 57–58, 78–79, 123–24, 129–30

de la Mare, Walter, 137

Dickens, Charles, 35, 52, 53, 59, 90, 94, 127

Donne, John, 6, 14, 127

Eliot, George, 31, 90

Eliot, T. S., 26, 31, 32, 36, 42, 46, 51, 62–63

Ellmann, Richard, 75

Ernst, Max, 42

Fernhill Farm, 2, 4, 7, 10, 15, 20, 22, 24, 135

Fitzgerald, F. Scott, 66–67, 99–100

Forster, E. M., 99–100

Graves, Robert, 11

Griffiths, Wyndham, 28

Gruffydd ap Adda, 133

haiku, 139, 140, 150
Hardy, Thomas, 11, 126
Hawkins, Desmond, 130
Heaney, Seamus, 5–6, 23, 79,
    151 (n. 2)
Herbert, George, 38, 62, 104
Hitchcock, Alfred, 102
Holiday, Billie, 145
Homer, 46, 57
Hopkins, Gerard Manley, 11,
    13–14, 34, 40–42, 49, 51, 52,
    53, 62, 81, 109, 140, 146
Hughes, Ted, 82–83
Hughes, Trevor, 7, 66, 67–69,
    128–31

Incledon, Walter, 26

James, Henry, 67, 102
Janes, Alfred (Fred), 27
Johnson, Pamela Hansford, 22–
    23, 27, 29, 43, 67, 68, 75, 130,
    138, 140
Jones, Ann, 7–9, 12–13, 14, 69,
    116–17, 148
Jones, Daniel, 57–58, 95–96
Jones, Kitty (née Janes), 27
Joyce, James, 2, 23, 30, 31, 34,
    35, 36, 37–38, 40–42, 46, 51,
    52, 53, 54–55, 56, 57, 59, 63–
    65, 66, 73–77, 81, 82, 89, 93,
    94, 96, 118–19, 120, 121, 134,
    137

Kant, Emmanuel, 71
Keats, John, 6, 9, 74, 88, 97, 98
Koestler, Arthur, 72

Laugharne, 4, 17, 19, 20, 72
Lawrence, D. H., 31, 33, 53, 113,
    117, 137, 144
Leavis, F. R., 28
Llywd, Alan, 11
Loesch, Katharine, 10, 32, 34
Longinus, 71–72

Mabinogion, 1
Magritte, René, 42, 43, 47, 50
Mansfield, Katherine, 54
Marvell, Andrew, 137
Maud, Ralph, 57–58, 78–79,
    123–24, 129–30
Messiaen, Olivier, 53
Mewslade, 29
Milton, John, 9, 15, 24, 82, 117,
    122, 134, 136–37
Ministry of Information, 61
Morgannwg, Iolo, 133

Nathan, Bill, 47

Owen, Wilfred, 11

Peach, Linden, 98
Picasso, Pablo, 42, 53
Plath, Sylvia, 84
Plato, 84
Price, Edmund (archdeacon of
    Merioneth), 13
Proust, Marcel, 90
Purcell, Henry, 40

Ransom, John Crowe, 137
Resnais, Alain, 105–6
Rhossilli, 29–30, 67–76, 145

Rhys, Keidrych, 68
Richardson, Dorothy, 35
Roughton, Roger, 26–27, 43, 128

Shakespeare, William, 34, 35, 37, 52, 53, 54–56, 62, 70–71, 86–87, 88, 115, 133
Shelley, Percy Bysshe, 9
Shklovsky, Victor, 138
Sillitoe, Alan, 90
South Wales Evening Post, 96
Spender, Stephen, 9, 151 (n. 2)
Spewack, Sam, 62
Stevens, Wallace, 26, 128–31, 136, 141
surrealism, 26, 43–44, 47

Tennyson, Alfred, Lord, 36
Thomas, Caitlin, 79–80
Thomas, D. J., 52, 67
Thomas, George, 33
Thomas, R. S., 3, 14
Thomas, Thomas, 28
Thomas, William, 10
Thomas, Wynn, 27

Treece, Henry, 31–32, 33, 43, 135
Treherne, Thomas, 132, 137
Twain, Mark, 73

Uplands, The (Swansea), 28

Vaughan, Henry, 137
Virgil, 105, 115

Wales, 68
Watkins, Vernon, 60, 103–5, 106, 108, 138, 141
Wilde, Jimmy, 79
Williams, Rhydwen, 11
Woolf, Virginia, 31, 33, 35, 37–38, 53, 115
Woolsey, John M., 57
Wordsworth, Dorothy, 146
Wordsworth, William, 20, 25, 51–52, 74, 88, 91–92, 118, 140, 150
Worm's Head, 29–30, 69–76

Yeats, W. B., 5, 6, 22, 73, 96, 103–4, 105, 109, 147